Integrating the

ARTS

Across the Elementary School Curriculum

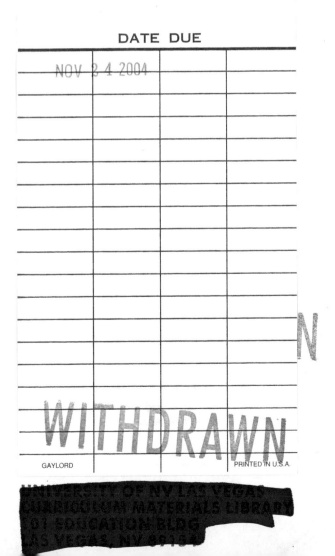

THOMSON

™

WADSWORTH

Publisher: **Edith Beard Brady**
Education Editor: **Dan Alpert**
Development Editor: **Tangelique Williams**
Editorial Assistant: **Heather Kazakoff**
Technology Project Manager: **Barry Connolly**
Marketing Manager: **Dory Schaeffer**
Marketing Assistant: **Neena Chandra**
Advertising Project Manager: **Shemika Britt**
Project Manager, Editorial Production:
 Trudy Brown

Print/Media Buyer: **Doreen Suruki**
Permissions Editor: **Kiely Sexton**
Production Service: **UG / GGS Information
 Services, Inc.**
Text and Cover Designer: **Garry Harman**
Copy Editor: **Julie Kennedy**
Compositor: **UG / GGS Information
 Services, Inc**
Text and Cover Printer: **Webcom**

For more information about our products, contact us at:
Thomson Learning Academic Resource Center
1-800-423-0563
For permission to use material from this text,
contact us by: **Phone:** 1-800-730-2214
Fax: 1-800-730-2215
Web: http://www.thomsonrights.com

Library of Congress Control Number:
2003103265

ISBN 0-534-61141-9

Wadsworth/Thomson Learning
10 Davis Drive
Belmont, CA 94002-3098
USA

Asia
Thomson Learning
5 Shenton Way #01–01
UIC Building
Singapore 068808

Australia/New Zealand
Thomson Learning
102 Dodds Street
Southbank, Victoria 3006
Australia

Canada
Nelson
1120 Birchmount Road
Toronto, Ontario M1K 5G4
Canada

Europe/Middle East/Africa
Thomson Learning
High Holborn House
50/51 Bedford Row
London WC1R 4LR
United Kingdom

Latin America
Thomson Learning
Seneca, 53
Colonia Polanco
11560 Mexico D.F.
Mexico

Spain/Portugal
Paraninfo
Calle/Magallanes, 25
28015 Madrid, Spain

To Dr. Kristen and her boys

CONTENTS _____

PREFACE

This book is designed to assist pre-service and in-service classroom teachers, specialists, curriculum consultants, and other educational personnel in ways of weaving music, art, drama, and movement/dance into the elementary and middle school curriculum to stimulate the learning process, enrich other subject areas, and provide valuable pathways for creative expression and self-fulfillment.

The intent is not to train artists; rather it is to aid educators in becoming "user friendly" with the creative arts through a blend of background information, activity ideas, and reassurance for those of timid persuasion that artistic talent is not a requirement for conducting rewarding arts experience in their classrooms. To that end, the book also seeks to:

1. intensify awareness of how arts experiences woven into educational fabric can motivate and reenforce learnings in other classroom disciplines,
2. provide terminology, basic skills, and content/methodology to facilitate planning procedures related to each art form, and
3. aid in exploring ways of translating such information into creative endeavors intended to further desired learnings.

ABOUT THIS BOOK

The book is organized around three major sections. Part I, The Power of the Arts, presents:

1. affirmations to the value of the arts drawn from recognized research and experienced educators
2. the nature of creativity, the importance of nurturing it in the classroom, and suggestions for helping students achieve their own creative potential
3. ways of becoming more comfortable with the arts and helping others to do the same

Part II, The Art Forms, addresses each art separately, providing:

1. background information (some historical), elements, materials, and processes related to the given art,
2. an abundance of activities—some intended for use in achieving desired goals at the training level, others for implementation in future classrooms

with children—all designed to increase student involvement and enhance learning

3. study questions to measure grasp of concepts and spark discussion, writing, and research as well as the creation of more activities

4. summary of the National Standards for the given art—upon which many of the stated activities are based

5. reading references and other resources, including Web sites and suppliers of specialized materials.

Part III, Integrating the Arts, "connects" the arts with other disciplines through:

1. activity ideas for integrating music, art, drama, and dance into other subjects such as social studies, science, mathematics, and language arts—including an extended section on various poetry forms

2. suggested ways of relating the arts to each other and to thematically focused topics

3. reports from teachers in service on successfully integrating projects conducted in their classrooms

For those who wish to pursue any of the arts in more depth, reading references and other helpful resources, including the locations of Web sites and suppliers of specialized materials, are also included throughout.

It should be noted that this book has been deliberately kept brief so as to increase its flexibility for use either as a main text or supplement, not only to accommodate a variety of institutional time frames (e.g., shortened semesters, abbreviated summer terms, etc.) but also their various levels of study, including undergraduate, graduate, certificate, and others.

Finally, the hope is that students will enjoy personally satisfying aesthetic experiences while simultaneously learning ways of helping children to do the same, and in the process, become increasingly aware not only of the intrinsic values of the arts but also of their power to interpret meaning.

ACKNOWLEDGMENTS _____

The author is deeply grateful to all who gave permission to reprint copyrighted and other material. Despite sincere and extended efforts, a few of the sources could not be uncovered. If there is a lack of proper acknowledgment in any place, it is only because the source is unknown. The author would appreciate being informed about any such instances in order that proper acknowledgment may be made and appropriate arrangements secured for any future editions.

The author wishes to thank Dan Alpert, Trudy Brown, and Kiely Sexton at Wadsworth. The author also thanks the following reviewers, whose thoughtful comments helped to improve this book:

Harlan Brownlee, University of Missouri-Kansas City
Sharon Crisman, Gannon University
Mark Graham, Washington State University
Mary Stone Hanley, University of North Carolina-Chapel Hill
Lora Lawson, Wittenburg University
Jo Ann N. Nelson, Southern Illinois University at Carbondale
Anne M. Slanina, Slippery Rock University
Sharon A. Stander, University of Nevada-Reno
Diana Suskind, Fitchburg State University
Yolanda M. Wattsjohnson, Marquette University
Stanley Wollock, William Patterson University

The author also wishes to acknowledge her gratitude for help and support from the following individuals:

Jennifer Fales
Arthur Guagliumi
Judith Lenzi-McGoveny
Marlene Wendt
Jacqueline Westphal
Nancy Whelan
Beth Wollar
Ali Zamouri

Introduction

Discovering Who We Are

The arts have been part of us from the very beginning. Since nomadic peoples first sang and danced for their ancestors, since hunters first painted their quarry on the walls of caves, since parents first acted out the stories of heroes for their children, the arts have described, defined and deepened human experience. All peoples, everywhere, have an abiding need for meaning—to connect time and space, experience an event, body and spirit, intellect and emotion. People create art to make these connections, to express the otherwise inexpressible. A society and a people without the arts are unimaginable. Such a society and people could not long survive.

The arts are one of humanity's deepest rivers of continuity. They connect each new generation to those who have gone before. . . . At the same time the arts are often an impetus for change, challenging old perspectives from fresh angles of vision, or offering original interpretations of familiar ideas. The arts disciplines provide their own ways of thinking, habits of mind. . . . At another level, the arts are society's gift to itself, linking hope to memory, inspiring courage, enriching our celebrations and making our tragedies bearable. The arts are also a unique source of enjoyment and delight, providing the "Aha!" of discovery when we see ourselves in a new way, grasp a deeper insight or find our imaginations refreshed. The arts have been a preoccupation of every generation precisely because they bring us face to face with ourselves, and with what we sense lies beyond ourselves. . . .

If our civilization is to continue to be both dynamic and nurturing, its success will ultimately depend on how we develop the capacities of our children, not only to earn a living in a vastly complex world, but to live a life rich in meaning. . . . A future worth having depends on being able to construct a vital relationship with the arts. . . .[1]

 or decades the arts have played a lesser than deserved role in the educational process—frequently designated as "frill," and even more frequently the first targeted elimination when school budgets tightened. Indeed, during those same decades, it appeared that school boards and others were simply not being convinced of the value of the arts in the learning process. What was needed, apparently, was mind-catching evidence from trusted establishments and resonating voices to get the good word out.

At last, it seems, help is on the way in the form of strong urgings from "respectable" sources validating what many knew all along—that the arts are vital to the education process. Such voices include those of Howard Gardner, Eric Jensen, and others, as well as national legislation in the form of Goals 2000: Educate America Act (passed March 1994) containing the National Standards for Arts Education.

National Standards for Arts Education

According to the National Standards Summary Statement, the National Standards for Arts Education is a statement of what every young American should know and be able to do in four arts disciplines—dance, music, theater and the visual arts—covering both content and achievement in grades K–12. The Summary Statement also assures us that "with the passage of the Goals 2000: Educate America Act, the national goals are written into law naming the arts as a core, academic subject—as important to education as English, mathematics, history, civics and government, geography, science and foreign language." These arts standards represent the combined efforts of the Music Educator's National Conference, the National Art Education Association, the National Dance Association, the American Alliance for Theatre & Education, and others who shared their thoughts on the project.

Inclusion of arts standards in the Educate America Act indicates an intensifying awareness of the value of the arts in the educational process—a fact duly noted by most of the states who are either in the process or have already produced their own arts standards.

A sampling of states representing different geographical areas of the country revealed similarities as well as differences in their wordings; however, most still reflected the spirit of the national framework.[2]

A few were written in very general terms and grouped grade levels into K–4, 5–8, and 9–12 in the same manner as the nationals. Others were more specific, and dealt with each grade level separately for all categories of learning. California included Pre-K. Texas showed no kindergarten. Texas also included a listing of specified courses from which schools could select. It was interesting to note that Texas chose to place Dance with the Physical Education Standards instead of with Arts.

North Carolina added more categories to its Standards and under Dance included a note to the effect that "the study of dance is cumulative and sequential to include learning from previous grade levels."

Pennsylvania's streamlined approach stated things more broadly—in statements applicable to all arts and selected grade levels. All of the states' standards viewed contained glossaries of terms relative to each art; however,

Pennsylvania's glossary consisted of terms used in the document (e.g., aesthetic criticism, critical analysis, and others).

Maryland designated the categories below as essential learner outcomes:

1. Perceiving and responding—aesthetic education
2. Historical, cultural, and social contexts
3. Creative expression and production
4. Aesthetic criticisms

Following each category, sample instructional activities for achieving stated expectations were suggested.

Some states (Texas, Arkansas, North Carolina, California) referred to "strands"—defined by Texas as providing "broad unifying structure for organizing the knowledge and skills students are expected to acquire."

New Hampshire defined proficiency standards as levels of achievement students are expected to attain at completion of grades 4, 8, and 12 and designated *creating, performing,* and *responding* as the three basic processes common to the arts.

Canada's standards were also viewed. Not surprising was the combining of drama and dance into one category because the two arts share many aspects in common. Of note from Canada was the inclusion in the document of the message to parents related to overall and specific outcomes, as well as notes on critical thinking.

In summary, the journey through states' standards proved an interesting one. In some of the samples viewed, the quality of the content represented careful thought, extensive preparation time born of deep commitment and great vision on the part of the producers. Others seemed to be content with the minimum.

One cannot help but speculate on whether the care given to the preparation of such a document might also be a reflection of the way a given state values its arts.

In fairness to the stiller, smaller voices, it should be noted here that despite the value of the standard as contributors to the cause, like many other governmental acts, they are not without their critics.

In her book *Creating Integrated Curriculum* Susan Drake maintains that "when we create standards we confront a fundamental question in education: What is worth knowing?"[3]

Speaking to the assessment issue implicit in all standards, Eric Jensen poses the question "ask not whether we can assess the arts but rather whether we should. . . ." and goes on to say that "arts are not for short term assessment . . . they are not about counting notes, brush strokes or dance steps. They are about life, growth and expanding who we can become as human beings." Jensen also reminds us that "not everything that's measurable is important, and not everything that's important is measurable."[4]

The word "measurable" reminds us that progress in the arts area is also being slowed by such factors as the emphasis on end-of-grade testing and the surging accountability movement—all of which can hamper the vision of administrators as well as teachers.

Other questions addressing the standards on a more practical note are being raised by arts educators themselves who, one may assume, will bear much of the burden of responsibility for implementation. Their main concerns translate into, "Thanks for our rightful place at last, but who's going to schedule, teach and fund all this?"

Whatever the concerns or answers are to all of the above, the hopes are that the arts have begun to achieve their long deserved recognition as core components of an education, and those of us who are committed to perpetuating their miracles are grateful.

— NOTES —

1. From *National Standards for Arts Education*, published by Music Educators National Conference (MENC). Copyright © 1994 by MENC. Used by permission. The complete National Arts Standards and additional materials relating to the Standards are available from MENC—The National Association for Music Education, 1806 Robert Fulton Drive, Reston, VA 20191 (telephone 800-336-3768).

2. For more information on state and Canadian arts standards please refer to the following:

California Department of Education
P. O. Box 944272
Sacramento, CA 94244-2720
Tel: 916-319-0791

Maryland Department of Education
200 West Baltimore St.
Baltimore, MD 21207
Tel: 410-767-0100

New Hampshire State Board and Department of Education
201 Pleasant St.
Concord, NH 03301
Tel: 603-271-3743

North Carolina Department of Public Instruction
301 N. Washington St.
Raleigh, NC 27601
Tel: 919-807-3300

Pennsylvania Department of Education
333 Market St.
Harrisburg, PA 17126
Tel: 717-783-6788

Texas Educational Agency
1701 North Congress Ave.
Austin, TX 78701-1494
Tel: 512-463-9734

Ontario Ministry of Education
Mowat Block 900 Bay St.
Toronto, Ontario M7A 1 L2 Canada
Tel: 416-325-2829 or 800-387-5514

3. Susan Drake, *Creating Integrating Curriculum* (Thousand Oaks, CA: Corwin Press, 1998). Reprinted by permission.

4. Eric Jensen, *Arts with the Brain in Mind* (Alexandria, VA: Association for Supervision and Curriculum Development, 2000).

BLESSED be the musicians of the world who sing out the song that fills my heart
BLESSED be the painters of the world who capture the forms and colors dancing
      behind my eyelids
BLESSED be the poets of the world who take the plain words from my lips and
      hurl them with their magic like sacred birds into the sky
BLESSED be the guardians of the legends and dreams for their music and words
      of love swell within my soul so that I may offer them like a prayer

Ojibwa Indian

PART I

The Power of the Arts

Arts in Education

What We Know

Experiencing an art for its own sake can be a joy in itself. Beyond this, bringing the arts into the educational setting allows them to manifest their full power. In the classroom, the arts can hold the potential for facilitating many of the desired goals that provide a basis for enhanced learning—specifically:

- Sharpening sensory awareness
- Improving verbal/nonverbal communication
- Enhancing collaborative/cooperative skills
- Stimulating the imagination
- Developing creative potential
- Refining auditory/visual skills
- Aiding practice in gross/fine motor skills
- Fostering cognitive, affective, kinesthetic, and aesthetic development
- Heightening sensitivity to diversity
- Providing emotional release and reducing stress
- Improving self-image
- Developing self-discipline

With so many activities from which to choose in each area, the presence of the arts greatly enhances the opportunities for all children to find their avenues of success leading to a large measure of self-fulfillment. Of particular importance are the benefits to those with low self-esteem and individuals with various physical/mental/emotional challenges who, despite limitations, can make significant contributions through the arts. In this connection, one teacher reported:

> As an art teacher I have observed many children who possess a natural talent in drawing and re-creating what they observe from nature and the world around them. I would never know that several of these students had learning disabilities, difficulty in reading and processing words and information.

According to the founder of the Nordoff-Robbins Music Therapy Clinic at New York University, children with cerebral palsy, Down's syndrome, and other challenging conditions may evidence remarkable ability in music—finding in its discipline not only a means for expression but also one that "brings order to their disorganized inner world."[1]

In the classroom arts play a vital part in the problem-solving process by strengthening the right or intuitive side of the brain to aid in finding alternative solutions and more creative thinking. Linda Williams, author of *Teaching for the Two Sided Mind* says, in part, that "children come with a two sided mind. We must encourage them to use it, to develop both types of thinking so that they have access to the fullest possible range of mental abilities."[2]

In *Arts with the Brain in Mind* Eric Jensen writes "evidence from brain research is only one of the many reasons to support the arts as an integral part of the educational process." He goes on to say that "the arts enhance the process of learning. The systems they nourish which include our integrated sensory attentional, cognitive, emotional and motor capacities are in fact the driving forces behind all other learning. . . ."[3]

Jensen also cites research of Judith Burton and others at Columbia University showing that subjects such as science, math, and language require complex cognitive and creative capacities "typical of arts learning." Reporting further on Burton's study of more than 2000 children, Jensen writes that "those in an arts curriculum were far superior in creative thinking, self-concept, problem-solving, self expression, risk taking and cooperation than those who were not."[4] In light of such studies, one might conceivably hypothesize that Einstein's early musical experience and Galileo's visual art training may have been contributing factors to their later creative thinking.

As noted above, apart from their intrinsic values, weaving arts experiences into the educational fabric can motivate, vitalize, and strengthen learnings in other classroom disciplines, frequently providing the point of entry through which the learning takes on meaning. Offering a broad spectrum of arts activities means providing more settings for teaching any given concept and more opportunities for learning reinforcement.

As an aid to helping children understand cultures different from their own, the arts can play a vital role not only in illuminating origins and customs, but also in awakening awareness of the universality of the human spirit. Moreover, the arts can help some children find their cultural identities and, in the process, improve multicultural understanding and an appreciation for ethnicity.

In classrooms where the arts are welcomed, teachers are in the enviable position of conceivably discovering young people who possess unusual talent as well as permitting a showcase for arts-related careers and possible present/future leisure-time pursuits. Improving the quality of leisure-time pursuits could conceivably result in improving the quality of life itself.

In summary, arts experiences can become efficient laboratories for developing creative problem-solving skills and abilities that will serve students long after formal training ends. In view of this, if the arts are to play the significant role they *should* to accomplish all the things they *can*, then ways must be found to integrate them into the total classroom curriculum as an accepted mode of learning.

What Others Say

One of the strongest validations for the inclusion of the arts in the educational process has appeared in the form of the theory of multiple intelligences advanced by Harvard professor Howard Gardner (Fig. 1.1). Disputing the

FIGURE 1.1

MULTIPLE INTELLIGENCES

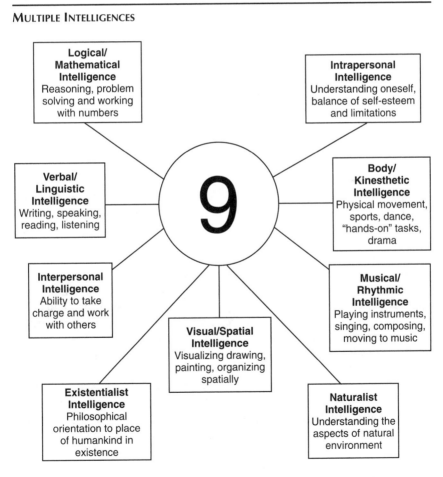

Logical/ Mathematical Intelligence
Reasoning, problem solving and working with numbers

Intrapersonal Intelligence
Understanding oneself, balance of self-esteem and limitations

Verbal/ Linguistic Intelligence
Writing, speaking, reading, listening

Body/ Kinesthetic Intelligence
Physical movement, sports, dance, "hands-on" tasks, drama

Interpersonal Intelligence
Ability to take charge and work with others

Musical/ Rhythmic Intelligence
Playing instruments, singing, composing, moving to music

Visual/Spatial Intelligence
Visualizing drawing, painting, organizing spatially

Existentialist Intelligence
Philosophical orientation to place of humankind in existence

Naturalist Intelligence
Understanding the aspects of natural environment

previously held notion that meaning is derived solely through analysis and reason, Gardner maintains that all human beings possess multiple intelligences. In his earlier studies he named seven: music, kinesthetic, language, visual, logic/math, interpersonal, and intrapersonal. Later on, two more were added: naturalist and existentialist. Present indications are that more may be yet to come and that some possible revision of those already named may also be under consideration. Designating the arts as intelligences has resulted in arousing awareness of their intrinsic worth as well as their importance in the learning process.

The advent of Gardner's work has precipitated some rethinking of the theories expressed by earlier pioneers such as Jean Piaget, known for his work on the development of cognitive abilities.

Whereas Piaget defined intelligence as an "adaptation" and characterized it as a single thing, Gardner holds that all normal human beings possess multiple forms of intelligence in different degrees, and that competence in one is not necessarily related to competence in the others. He defines intelligence as "an ability to solve problems or to fashion a product, to make something that is valued in at least one culture."[5]

Piaget divided children's mental growth into stages:

- Sensory-motor (birth–2 years)
- Pre-operational (2–7 years)
- Concrete operational (7–12 years)
- Formal operational (12–15 years)

with each stage fairly defined as to its anticipated capabilities upon which the next stage would be built.[6]

According to Gardner, accepting Piaget's theory of a single intelligence means believing that "if a person were at one level of understanding he would be of the same level of understanding every kind of material dealt with." In other words, "if a person is concrete operational with one thing, he is concrete operational with everything else, and those who pass through Piaget's stages more quickly than others would be considered the 'bright people.' "

In the course of his work, Gardner came in contact with many varied populations in which he saw individuals with strengths in one area, but noted that such strengths did not predict whether they would be strong in other areas. In Gardner's words, "most children have very 'jagged profiles'—profiles that are much more complex than the standard intelligence á la Piagetian theory would allow." In addition, Gardner cites exceptional populations as being very difficult to explain using the standard intelligence theory and impossible to explain via Piaget . . . "one of whose principal claims is essentially disconfirmed by every prodigy and every autistic individual." In this connection, a special education teacher in a university graduate seminar shared her concerns:

I am continuously involved in evaluating youngsters who are under consideration for special services. Conventional tests and achievement batteries are given to determine eligibility for special education services. . . . I am befuddled at times by a student's "high" or "low" IQ scores and the contradiction of academic performance in the classroom. The IQ score is by no means a portrait of the learner in my classroom. Children do best when offered learning options that capitalize on their strengths. . . . Intelligence is not a figure but a compilation of talents.

In his book *Frames of Mind*, Gardner writes "each intelligence has its own ordering mechanism, and the way that an intelligence performs its ordering reflects its own principles and its own preferred media."[7]

It is Gardner's contention that all of these intelligences should be acknowledged when designing learning experiences; otherwise, those who do not excel in the "traditional" intelligences may be deprived of needed support. Moreover, Gardner urges matching children to "congenial approaches of teaching, learning and assessing" to increase the likelihood of their achieving "educational success." To facilitate this, Gardner says educators should take note of individual differences in order to "personalize instruction and assessment."

Strong supporters of Gardner, such as Thomas Armstrong, argue that the emphasis on instruction and testing on only two of the intelligences—language and logic—has resulted in some children being labeled as "deficient" when, in fact, it is the teaching that is at fault—not the children.

Assuming that all education should include the arts as cognitive domains or forms of understanding, advocates of Gardner's theories maintain that there is power in education *through* the arts as well. The argument is that if a student cannot comprehend traditional academic subjects verbally or linguistically, that student can understand them visually, musically, or even kinesthetically. In Susan Stinson's words, "A child who demonstrates considerable bodily-kinesthetic intelligence would be able to learn mathematical concepts through whole body activities and likely be more successful at it."[8] Commenting on Gardner's theories, Ormrod observes that "These intelligences identified by Gardner may manifest themselves in different ways in various cultures."[9]

In summary, the implication of Gardner's theories for educators are that:

- Children should be recognized as capable in ways other than those on which schools traditionally base assessment and
- The inclusion of arts-related areas among the designated intelligences sends a clear message that arts experiences must be provided in the classroom lest children be deprived of some of their learning tools.

Implementing Gardner's Theories

As one teacher put it, "it takes time, patience, creativity, and hard work." She was of course referring to putting Gardner's theories into practice in the classroom. To do this means moving beyond the familiar to the challenging—becoming more aware of ways to identify individual intelligences, then designing projects to address them.

In the process, there may be a need to reevaluate how information is presented and learning assessed, taking care that activities and evaluative instruments chosen will fairly allow students to bring their personal gifts into play. In short, targeted learnings must be interwoven in such a way that each student has the opportunity to experience and absorb them through a variety of channels.

Understandably, teachers who feel insecure about their own strengths in a particular art may be apprehensive about conducting activities related to it. For those the message is twofold: First, believe you can, and then call upon available specialists as well as parents and other community resources for additional ideas. Many are delighted to be asked and talents abound. In addition, the Internet is laden with information that can spark a teacher's own undiscovered creativity.

Implementing Gardner's theories may exemplify the old saying that the journey is its own reward. Accomplishing this task could conceivably require many hours of solitary as well as cooperative planning—sharing ideas with other educators, risk taking among the new and untried, and challenging confrontations with old habits and boundaries. There are those who will say we should have been doing this all along.

In addition to Gardner, other advocates for the arts in education speak to us from a wide variety of settings. For example, Stephanie Perrin, author of *Education in the Arts Is an Education for Life*, maintains that serious study of the arts is one of the best ways to educate a young person for college and employment. According to Perrin, research at schools that devote 25 percent or more of the curriculum to arts courses shows that students in such schools acquire academically superior abilities. Citing the relationship between learning in the arts and academic learning, Perrin maintains that the power of the arts is one avenue for learning that we should explore.[10]

Reporting on an arts-integrated school, one researcher notes that "through the arts the whole school 'ecology' changes" and "not only do the arts enable students to achieve academically at rates far beyond what might be expected of them (in subjects such as math and science) but other marvelous things happen as well." Notable among the marvels are increased motivation to learn, respect for peers, enhanced relationships between students and teachers, as well as an improved work ethic where high standards become the norm.

In a *Kappan* article titled "What Do We Want Our Schools to Do?" Eric Oddleifson quotes Ron Berger, a teacher in an arts integrated school who reported that "the infusion of arts has had a profound effect on student understanding, investment and standards," and that students do well not only on "standardized testing measures but also in real-life measures of learning."[11]

In a private conversation with Oddleifson, physicist Morton Tavel of Vassar College expressed his belief that the "future of the sciences is dependent on the arts." Citing Einstein's suggestion that the very purpose of science is to understand the senses, Tavel states that the arts have similar aims. "The sciences and the arts are both investigations into the nature of reality. . . . Artists and scientists share the desire to investigate and express the ways interlocking pieces of reality fit together." The differences lie simply in the symbol systems and verification of conclusions.

Leonard Shlain, author of *Arts and Physics*, suggests that the arts "are primary sources of material with which to engage in scientific thinking. Moreover, they provide connections that allow lateral leaps between cognitive domains which can produce sudden scientific insight."[12]

Biology teacher Karen Gallas reports great success incorporating Gardner's philosophy into her classroom where students are required to "observe and record the anatomy and physiology of insects" but where they are also encouraged to present their findings through whatever medium they chose. "One child wrote a poem imagining life as an ant, while others drew or acted out what they learned." Results showed a "much deeper assimilation of the basic concepts than conventional rote memorization." According to Gallas, "knowing isn't just telling something back as we receive it. It means transformation and change."[13]

Biochemist Robert Root-Bernstein feels that contributions of the arts to science and technology are long overdue, and writes that "experiments alone cannot produce conceptual breakthroughs . . . one must first be able to imagine that which is to be tested and how to test it. . . . By first approaching a problem visually, the scientist builds a mental construct that later can be translated into some verbal or mathematical form."[14]

AT&T executive Morris Tannenbaum, addressing a National Arts Convention, is quoted as saying, "Tomorrow's scientists and engineers need grounding in the arts to stimulate their curiosity and creativity—to help them perceive the world in new and different ways. . . . In the final analysis, though the best reason for bringing the arts and sciences together might be to make learning more fun in the process." He goes on to say that "art and science are of a piece; the methods differ but the game is the same. Or, as Arthur Koestler noted, 'Newton's apple and Cezanne's apple are discoveries more closely related than they seem.' "[15]

Richard Gurin, president and CEO of Binney and Smith Inc., expressed a growing consensus among business leaders. "After a long business career I have become increasingly concerned that the basic problem gripping the American workplace is . . . the crisis of creativity. Ideas are what built American business and it's the arts that build ideas and nurture a place in the mind for them to grow. Arts education programs can help repair weakness in American education and better prepare workers for the twenty-first century."[16]

Gurin is just one of many arts advocates around the country who are forming arts/business partnerships to bring business leaders, arts organizations, and educators together to address the same fundamental message that "an education in the arts opens the door to skills and abilities that equip learners for a host of learning contexts, including the workplace where knowledge is wealth." The consensus is that "today's and tomorrow's workers have to be multi-skilled and multi-dimensional, flexible and intellectually supple."

The concerns of business leaders also encircle the widening global workscape, pointing up the need for a greater understanding not only of various languages but also of "world cultures, traditions and histories." Because the arts speak to all cultures, "they offer an obvious attraction."

MIT associate provost for the arts Ellen Harris reports that the arts have helped prepare MIT students in business:

> An alumnus at a large New York accounting firm recently stated at an MIT alumni meeting that his firm interviews about forty MIT students every year. Of the ones they recently hired, four presented minors in the arts. The latter fact so significantly set these candidates apart from the others in terms of creative thinking, flexibility and presentation that the firm is now using the arts minor as a screening criterion.[17]

Miller and Coen report a survey by the late physician and biologist Lewis Thomas revealing that of the medical students who majored in biochemistry as undergraduates, 44 percent were admitted to medical school. In contrast, 66 percent of those who majored in music as undergraduates gained admission—the highest percentage for any undergraduate major. It was Thomas's belief that "medical schools want to admit people who are steeped in the liberal arts and capable of relieving stress through music, acting, dancing, sculpting and other arts . . . so that a student who would be a physician will first grow as a human being."[18]

In conclusion, an optimistic note from Morris Tannenbaum:

> If the arts can get a foot in the door, if we can stop looking at science as just so many formulas to learn or numbers to tote up, then perhaps we can get on with putting a sense of awe and wonder back into education.

FOR FURTHER STUDY

1. Some individuals seem to feel alienated toward the arts and uncomfortable at the thought of participating in an arts experience. Comment on what you feel might be possible reasons for this. Can you recall some of your earlier experiences/feelings related to the arts that may have affected your present attitude?

2. Confer with arts educators and other school personnel in public and private schools in your community to learn what part, if any, the arts are currently playing in attaining the stated educational objectives.

3. Research more on the learning theories touched upon in this chapter, then:
   a. Explain in specific terms the significance of these theories as related to the inclusion of the arts in the classroom curriculum.

   b. As a small-group project, create an imaginary conversation between
      Jean Piaget and Howard Gardner, considering salient points of their
      theories, agreements, disagreements, and other information you deem
      pertinent. Assign roles, set a mandatory time limit, and play out for the
      class.

      (**Note:** Presentation should be organized in such a way that it contains
      a well-defined beginning, middle, and end.)

4. Investigate ways in which the arts are being used in:
   a. Health-care facilities for promoting better mental and/or physical
      health.
   b. Business and industry to improve managerial skills and increase
      productivity.
   c. Agriculture for achieving desired goals such as increased yield.
   d. Settings other than those noted above.

Getting Comfortable with the Arts

To many of us the word *arts* may evoke a gamut of emotions—from pleasurable to painful—depending upon our previous arts-related experiences. If we
were told in our early school years to "move your mouth but don't sing" or
that both our feet were of the left variety, then, understandably, such memo-
ries can cause enough lingering hurt to produce feelings of alienation toward
the arts throughout our lives.

   In view of this, and in the hope that such evils will not be perpetuated, it is
urged that arts activities be nourished in a nonthreatening, nonjudgmental
classroom climate wherein all learners feel free to share their gifts of ideas/
performance—however humble—without fear of failure. In this connection,
we must be aware that when we offer experiences—such as those in the arts,
for example—that are explored initially outside traditional rules/techniques
boundaries, the common definitions of success and failure do not apply.

   The educational value of the arts lies in the process—not the product;
thus, the intent is not to train artists; rather, it is to affirm the power of the
arts as a learning tool and a vital force in human existence. Such a commitment should extend to developing human beings into more fulfilled individuals and creative problem solvers destined to make significant contributions to
their own lives and the lives of others.

   When teachers are motivated to initiate efforts toward expanding arts involvement in their classrooms, they may be assured that not only will learning be enhanced, but also that an enriching dimension will be added to the
lives of young learners as well as to their own.

   Finally, it should be noted that a teacher need not be an artist, musician,
dancer, or other arts professional in order to provide a nurturing arts climate
that will vitalize the learning process. To that end, the materials that follow

were chosen for their ease of presentation and are directed toward deepening the comfort level of those individuals who perceive themselves as afflicted with "limited arts experience."

— NOTES —

1. Nordoff Robbins Music Therapy Clinic

   New York University
   26 Washington Place, New York, NY 10003
   Tel: (212) 998-5151

2. Linda Williams, *Teaching for the Two Sided Mind. A Guide to Right Brain/Left Brain Education* (New York: Simon & Schuster, 1983).

3. Eric Jensen, *Arts with the Brain in Mind* (Alexandria, VA: Association for Supervision and Curriculum Development, 2001).

4. J. Burton, R. Horowitz, and H. Abeles, "Learning in and Through the Arts: Curriculum Implications." In *Champions of Change: The Impact of the Arts on Learning,* ed. E. Fiske. (Online report.) (Washington, DC: The Arts Education Partnership and the President's Committee on the Arts and the Humanities, 1999). Available: http://www.artsedge.kennedy-center. org/champions/

5. Howard Gardner, "Multiple Intelligence: Implications for Art and Creativity." In *Artistic Intelligences: Implications for Education*, ed. William J. Moody (New York: Teachers College Press, 1990).

6. Jean Piaget, *The Origins of Intelligence in Children* (New York: W. W. Norton, 1963).

7. Howard Gardner, *Frames of Mind*, 2nd ed. (New York: Basic Books, 1993).

8. Susan Stinson, "Dance and the Developing Child." In *Moving and Learning for the Young Child*, ed. W. H. Stinson (Reston, VA: 1990). American Alliance for Health, Physical Education, Recreation and Dance.

9. Jeanne Ellis Ormrod, *Educational Psychology* (Columbus, OH: Merrill Publishing, 2000).

10. Stephanie Perrin, "Education in the Arts Is an Education for Life," *Phi Delta Kappan,* vol. 75 (February 1994).

11. Eric Oddleifson, "What Do We Want Our Schools to Do?" *Phi Delta Kappan*, vol. 75 (February 1994).

12. Leonard Shlain, *Art and Physics: Parallel Visions in Space, Time and Light* (New York: William Morrow, 1991).

13. Miriam Horn and Jill Sieder, "Looking for a Renaissance," *U. S. News and World Report* (March 30, 1992).

14. Robert Root-Bernstein, Report in *Brain Mind Bulletin* (July 1985).
15. *Why Do We Need the Arts* (New York: ACA Books, 1989).
16. Richard Gurin, "Educating for the Workplace through the Arts," *Business Week* (October 28, 1996).
17. Ellen T. Harris, "Why Study the Arts—Along with Math and Science?" *Aspen Institute Quarterly* (Winter 1992).
18. Allan Miller and Dorita Coen, "The Case for Music in the Schools," *Phi Delta Kappan* (February 1994).

— FOR FURTHER READING —

Alperstein, C., and R. B. Wely. *Arts for Everykid, A Handbook for Change.* Trenton, NJ: New Jersey State Council on the Arts and the Alliance for Art Education, 1992.

Berg, Geri, ed. *The Visual Arts and Medical Education.* Carbondale, IL: Southern Illinois University Press, 1983.

Beyond the Three R's—Transforming Education with the Arts Special Report. Educational Leadership, Oct. 1995.

Christoplos, F., and P. J. Valletutt. *Developing Children's Thinking Through the Arts.* Bloomington, IN: Phi Delta Kappan Educational Foundation, 1990.

Cornett, Claudia. *The Arts as Meaning Makers,* Prentice Hall Inc., A Pearson Education Company, 2000.

Dimondstein, G. *Exploring the Arts with Children.* New York: Macmillan, 1974.

Edwards, Linda Carol. *The Creative Arts*: *A Process Approach for Teachers and Children*, 3rd ed. Upper Saddle River, NJ: Merrill Prentice Hall, 2002.

Eloquent Evidence: Arts at the Core of Learning. Report of President's Committee on the Arts and Humanities and the National Assembly of State Arts Agencies. Washington, DC: Oct. 1995.

Fowler, C. *Strong Arts, Strong Schools.* Educational Leadership, Nov. 1994.

———. *Can We Rescue the Arts for America's Children?* New York: ACA Books, 1988.

Fulghum, Robert. *All I Really Need to Know I Learned in Kindergarten.* New York: Villard Books, 1989.

Gallas, Karen. *Languages of Learning.* New York: Teachers College Press.

Gardner, Howard. *Art, Mind and Brain.* New York: Basic Books, 1982.

———. *Frames of Mind.* New York: Basic Books, 1983.

———. *Multiple Intelligences: The Theory in Practice.* New York: Basic Books, 1993.

Mayesky, Mary. *Creative Activities for Young Children*. New York: Delmar, 1998.

Root-Bernstein, M. M. *Arts Are the 4th R in Education*. Lansing State Journal, 2 Dec. 1997.

Videos

Alternative Medicine: The Healing Arts. Princeton, NJ: Films for Humanities and Sciences, 1996.

Arts for Life. Paul Getty Trust, Getty Center for the Arts, 1990.

Teaching In and Through the Arts. Santa Monica, CA: Getty Center for the Arts, 1995.

2

Exploring Creativity

Arts and Creativity in the Classroom

A mind, stretched to a new idea never goes back to its original dimensions.

Oliver Wendell Holmes

To "create" means to "bring into being." In his definition of an artist, William Faulkner designated "everyone who has tried to create something which was not here before him, with no other tools and materials than the uncommerciable ones of the human spirit."

Furthering children's understanding of this concept means seeking out all available avenues of music, art, drama, dance, and other related arts to enable young people to bring their own creations into being as well as to deepen their appreciation for the creations of others.

Studies indicate that creating successfully in any field depends to a great extent upon the individual's fund of information in that field; therefore, we may assume that the greater store of experiences with which children have been provided, the better equipped they will be to produce substantial creations of their own. In Alane Starko's words, "When we teach to enhance creativity we may well be creative as teachers, but we also provide students the knowledge, skills and surroundings necessary for their own creativity to emerge." Starko also believes that students become "problem solvers and communicators rather than simply knowledge absorbers when exposed to learning activities designed to foster creativity."[1]

Howard Gardner defines a creative individual as a person "who regularly solves problems, fashions products or defines new questions in a domain in a way that is initially considered novel, but that ultimately becomes accepted in a particular culture setting."[2] Acknowledging that his definition of creativity parallels his definition of intelligence, Gardner believes that a person is creative "in a domain." Gardner's view of creativity is supported by that of

Albert Rothenberg, who defines creativity as the "ability to use different modes of thought."[3]

Jerome Bruner writes that creativity is "an act that produces effective surprise . . ." what he calls the "hallmark of a creative enterprise."[4]

Some researchers feel that anything designated creative must be classified as new or original. Others hold that creativity is not a product but a process in which old ideas are simply put together in new ways.

> That which has been, it is that which shall be; and that which has been done is that which shall be done, and there is nothing new under the sun.

> Ecclesiastes—1:9–10

Not quite so ancient are the thoughts of the poet Goethe:

> Everything has been thought of before. The problem is to think of it again.

Despite foregoing variant definitions, there appears to be general agreement that for optimum creative results the brain must be operating on both of its channels—left and right. We call upon the *left* side for logical thinking, speech, hearing, reading, writing, math, analyzing, verbal memory, reasoning, judgment, using symbols, and managing time. The *right* side provides us with spatial perception, visualizing, synthesizing, visual memory, insight, intuition, seeing whole things at once, and understanding analogies and metaphors and gut-level feelings. Both sides are important (Figure 2.1).

In *Sparks of Genius* Robert and Michele Root-Bernstein write:

> Whether we are attempting to understand ourselves, other people or some aspect of nature or simply provide excellent medical care, it is imperative that we learn to use the feelings, emotions and intuitions that are the bases of the creative imagination.[5]

Our present educational system is often viewed as not providing for sufficient use of the right brain. "Unfortunately," says one author, "most of our education is done by left brain types who, in turn, produce more left brain types." The consensus is that present-day education is smothering creativity. Tests show that a child's creativity plummets 90 percent between ages five

FIGURE 2.1

Frank and Ernest

and seven—a sign that education in its present form has neither helped each child maintain his or her precious sense of wonder nor provided the proper climate for its survival.[6]

Of interest are the findings that the childhoods of creative people were often beset by hardships ranging from financial woes to divorce and other familial dysfunctions. The belief held by some is that adversity may enhance the ability to see things from a different point of view.

Creative people tend to view things differently—like the bald man who was quoted as saying, "I'm not bald. I'm just taller than my hair." Lord Chesterfield observed that from a hayloft a horse looks like a violin. William James remarked that "Genius, in truth, means little more than perceiving in an unhabitual way." In one of his charming vignettes author Robert Fulghum, who writes of "common things in uncommon ways," gave us a new and respectful perspective on the lowly dandelion.

Creative people also see connections between seemingly unrelated things. Combining existing elements in new ways—a process known as *synergy*—has produced many innovations in the past, including the printing press, fork lift, circular saw, and others. *Serendipity*—making unexpected discoveries of things we are not looking for while searching for something else—also plays a part in the creative act because it relies on the awareness of relevance. For any discovery to be meaningful, it has to fall on a receptive mind—fertile with imagination—one that can make the appropriate connections. As Louis Pasteur put it, "Chance favors the prepared mind."

"Creative accidents" or mistakes have spawned numerous inventions. The impact of imaginative dreamer Albert Einstein's math formulas is well known to all. Not so familiar, perhaps, is the name of Roy Plunkett, referred to as the "Christopher Columbus of chemists," who bungled attempts to improve refrigeration technology and came up with Teflon instead.[7] Other such creative accidents include radar, penicillin, X-ray, Velcro, the microwave oven, and Post-its—all of which resulted from individuals making connections not previously seen by others. The "creative insight" of these discoverers allowed them to see what they were not looking for. Galileo reminds us, "Yet it often happens that we do not see what is quite near at hand and clear." To improve our creativity potential we must heighten our awareness, especially of what is relevant.

Creativity also requires that we be risk takers. Michael LeBoeuf, author of *Imagineering*, reports regretfully that "More good creative ability is wasted due to fear than anything else. People with good voices are afraid to sing, those with artistic talents hide their paintings rather than risk ridicule, writers are too embarrassed to show their writing to anyone."[8] Helen Keller put it a different way: "Life is either a daring adventure or nothing." In summary, we need to slay more dragons. Believing in our capacity for creative endeavor is a self-fulfilling prophecy.

Creative ideas find homes in unlikely as well as unusual places. Stephen Jay Gould writes of an "unforgettable visit" to a recycling market of Nairobi, Kenya, where "old telephone wire becomes jewelry, tin cans get sawed in half to be used as kerosene lamps, oil drum tops are beaten into large cooking pans, and treadless automobile tires become sturdy sandals."[9]

Heeding the charge to recycle, schools are finding multiple uses for what might be considered "industrial scrap"—discarded wood, plastic, and paper and other remnants unusable by the manufacturer and free for the asking. Such scrap has found a home among imaginative teachers who use it in various ways such as creating rain sticks from pvc pipes, drums, "found art" projects, and others.

It is now generally accepted that creativity can be taught; thus, it is important for children to learn that creative people are not necessarily limited to those who display special talents, and for teachers to know that everyone has some degree of creative potential that can flourish when given the proper spark and environment.

When attempting to stimulate creativity, the emphasis must be more on the *process* than on the final product. Therein, it would seem, lie the implications for the key role of the educator. What can be done to stimulate the process?

Among the traits found in creative individuals is a *strong sensory awareness*; thus, a good beginning is a sharpening of the sensory equipment—creating an awareness of the need to become better observers, listeners, tasters, smellers, and feelers. Michael LeBoeuf writes,

> Highly creative people . . . observe in greater detail and take in much more of the unique aspects of their environment. They also see more differences and similarities than the average person and bring more facts to bear on one aspect of a problem because they have perceived more through their senses. . . .[10]

Most adults are too closed to sensory impressions, tending to travel through life on "automatic pilot," as it were. We need to get in touch with our senses because they hold the key to richer awareness and empathy. Reminder: We were given two ears but only one mouth. "The arts . . . more than any other subject, awaken all the senses . . . the pores of learning."

Experiencing music, art, drama, dance, poetry, and other arts will not only help children become more sensorially aware but also will serve to stimulate their imaginations to see beyond what is merely apparent. Think on this:

> We hear but do we listen
> We look but do we see
> Not only what it is
> But what it could be

To further nourish our creative potential we must learn to ask, investigate, explore, search, experiment, and of course, *imagine*. Imagination is a different way of looking—a "willing suspension of disbelief." Einstein tells us that "Imagination is more important than knowledge." Mark Twain warns that "You can't depend on your judgment when your imagination is out of focus." When we imagine, we extend our vision and increase our openness, as well as our sensitivity to the concerns of other human beings.

An aid to developing our imaginations is to *think like a child*. One five-year-old described the moon as "God's big flashlight." Another determined that a caterpillar is simply "a worm with a sweater on." Children have no difficulty relating how it would feel to be a flower or a fox or even what the mental state of the turkey might be around Thanksgiving.

During an interview in which Steven Spielberg was asked how he came up with ideas for his works, he answered simply, "We're just a bunch of sappy kids fooling around a table." Woody Allen observed that humorists always sit at the children's table.

Playfulness is also considered an asset to creativity. Piaget termed play a strengthener of mental skills.[11] Viola Spolin writes that "everyone can learn through playing. Play touches and stimulates vitality, awakening the whole person—mind and body, intelligence and creativity, spontaneity and intuition. . . ." She also considers play (where social skills are learned) as one of the "few places where children can contribute to the adult controlled world" in which there is "little opportunity to accept community responsibility."[12] From the mouths of babes, an eight-year-old boy remarked to a student teacher, "It's surprising what we know when we've finished playing."[13]

In their book *Sparks of Genius*, authors Root-Bernstein quote Arthur Molella, director of the Smithsonian Institution Lamelson Center, as saying that "the sense of play is the essence of inventive activity." They also cite artist Alexander Calder who invented things because "it was fun, not to improve anyone" and Edward Lear who "played with words, invented new spoonerisms and punned endlessly. . . . Even Mozart and Bach played games with their music that mimicked pattern games played with words. . . . What charms us about a Mozart . . . or Calder is the fact that in some way they never grew up."[14] Perhaps the same may be said today of author Sark whose poster "How to Be an Artist"* tells us how in whimsical ways, including:

". . . entertain your inner child . . ."

". . . make little signs that say 'yes' and post them all over your house"

". . . hug trees . . ."

It would seem that those who bless us with creations that nourish the soul never lost their childlike sense of wonder. Have we too quickly forgotten how to play?

Comedy writers look at common things in uncommon ways and come up with the unexpected. That's what makes us laugh. Someone once conceived what might have been comments from spouses of famous people: From Louis Pasteur's wife, "I liked the taste of the milk better before you started fooling around with it." From Francis Scott Key's wife, "Why don't you write something we can sing sitting down?!" An assignment to college

Reprinted with permission from How to Be an Artist poster, copyright 1990 by SARK. Permission granted by Celestial Arts, P.O. Box 7123, Berkeley, CA 94707.

students to select a well-known person, then originate comments that could have emanated from his/her spouse yielded the following:

Noah's wife: "Explain to me again why we don't need an in-ground pool?"

Monet's wife: "Man, you need glasses!"

Children will produce even more insightful creations.

As teachers, if we hope to develop creativity in children, we can begin by becoming pathfinders ourselves—paying special attention along the route to our own need to:

- Sharpen sensory awareness
- Develop a sense of humor
- Take more risks
- Perceive things in a different way
- Make new connections between unconnected things
- Use more imagination
- Think like a child
- Become more playful
- Break out of old habits
- Practice empathy
- Be more open to change

"Change is a door that can be opened only from the inside," says an old French expression. Ingrained habits can be limiting to incoming ideas and creative thinking. When problem solving, we can begin by freeing our minds of existing rigid notions that bind us to ways it always *has been* and instead focus on what it *could be*—transforming traditional modes of thinking into new ways of looking at a given problem. Divergent or "lateral" thinking, as Edward deBono terms it, means digging more holes—as opposed to "vertical" thinking, meaning simply digging the same hole deeper.[15]

Finally, we need to be more passionate about what we do. Tom Peters, noted business consultant and author, notes that "the final connection among excellent companies are those in which the leaders unleash excitement."[16] It's been shown that the love we feel for our work can have a significant effect on the creativity of our performance. Confucius put it wisely: "Choose a job you love and you'll never have to work a day in your life."

While it is agreed that arts experiences in the classroom can foster the ability to think creatively, the success of any creative activity may be in large part dependent upon the atmosphere the teacher has created in the classroom. If all children have been made to feel that their contributions are welcome and worthy, then the climate is fertile for creative thinking. In contrast, an environment disquieted by tension and shattered dignities will destroy any kind of creative effort. Hiam Ginott puts it best:

> I've come to the frightening conclusion that I am the decisive element in the classroom. It's my personal approach that creates the climate. It's my daily mood that

makes the weather. As a teacher, I possess a tremendous power to make a child's life miserable or joyous. I can be a tool of torture or an instrument of inspiration. I can humiliate or humor, hurt or heal. In all situations, it is my response that decides whether a crisis will be escalated or de-escalated and a child humanized or dehumanized.[17]

A book on business management contains a chapter titled, "All Progress Depends on Those Who Color Outside the Lines." Creative people tend not to stay inside the lines, either on paper or in life. Often termed "mavericks," they come in all sizes. In the classroom they are not always the best behaved. When they appear before us as learners, we should be there not to negate but to nourish. In this connection, Joyce Boorman quotes a child cited in E. McIlveen's book *Cotton Candy Chatterbox* as saying, "You don't see me. You see only my skin, hair and eyes. The real me is hiding down in the cellar and I won't come out until I know you won't embarrass me."[18] In response, Boorman writes, "If they have to build that fortress, that citadel, to defend their creativity, our children may emerge later as the adolescent, the university student we teach, the adult mistakenly labeled as 'lacking in creativity.' When this occurs we have to go on that archeological dig, using all the tools and techniques available to us, to help bring that creativity out of the fortress where the child buried it for safety."[19]

> What you think of me
> I'll think of me
> And what I think of me
> I'll be.
>
> Anon

FOR DISCUSSION

1. With a notebook in hand, take an awareness walk in an area of your choice and pretend that you are seeing everything for the first time. Observe closely all the common things so often ignored—the design of a leaf, the contour of a tree, the color of a stone, and more. Make notes on everything you see, hear, and touch, as well as your reaction to the experience.

2. Summarize the characteristics of a creative person as cited by several different authors in selected readings. Identify those you feel you now possess as well as others that need more work. Design a plan for yourself that you consider suitable for achieving the desired results, stating your course of action in specific terms. (Note: Consider devising a type of format that would communicate the information to a reader in a more efficient way than simply a page of text.)

3. How would you define a creative teacher?

4. Describe what you feel would constitute a creative classroom climate. Be specific.

Activities

The activities suggested below are intended as examples of ways to initiate the process of exploring some aspects of creativity potential. It is intended that they be experienced first in the college classroom, then adapted as desired for future use with children in appropriate grade levels. Teachers may also identify uses in connection with other classroom disciplines as well.

Name Game

Depending on the size of the class, form several groups and sit in circles. Designate one person in each group as the lead-off person who says his/her first name accompanied by a descriptive adjective that begins with the same letter as the name, for example, "laughing Lisa" (or "Lisa the laughing"). Each person in turn then says the previous person's name and adjective followed by his/her own name and adjective (laughing Lisa, terrific Tom, etc.). This game may be repeated on another day with different groupings to facilitate learning more names. The same adjectives may be used or different ones chosen.

Stimulating the Imagination

1. Depending on the size of your class, form into groups of five to six people. Pass out index cards (one to each group) with three unrelated words written on each card. Sample words might be:
refrigerator, cat, car;
pail, basket, hat;
and others. (Words should be different on each card.) Ask groups to find connections between the words, then share findings with class. After each group presentation, invite additional ideas from the class on possible connections of the given words.

2. Form groups and pass out cards as before. Write on each card: What could you do if you were _____. Words to put in blanks include "invisible," "taller than anyone on earth," "able to move the clouds," and others.

3. Form groups and pass out cards as before. Write on each card: Find other uses for _____. Fill the blank on each card with a different object, for example, a plastic mixing bowl, a cardboard tube, Velcro, and others.

4. Form groups as before. Ask each group to choose any object, then find ways to modify it for a different use than it was originally intended, for example, increasing or diminishing its size, changing its shape, or adding something to it.

5. Form groups as before. Ask each group to come up with a definition for any one of the following contrived words: sluggestion, egonomics, wordscape. Have groups make up their own new words and definitions.

6. Have the whole class form a circle. Pass around a slipper and ask each person to demonstrate a different use for it. (Other objects may be substituted for the slipper.)

7. After reading comments from wives of famous persons (pp. 25–26), write new comments that might have been spoken by husbands or wives of famous people to their spouses.

Observing

1. Line up five people facing away from the instructor. The first one in line faces the instructor to receive five different gestures (point to chin, salute, etc.)—performed only once, slowly. The receiver waits until the instructor has completed all five, then passes them on to the next person—taking care to include all the gestures in the same sequence. The observing class is expected to note which, if any, gestures were omitted or altered in some way.

2. Form pairs. Look closely at each other to discern details in appearance, clothing, and other items. Have one person close his/her eyes while the other makes some minor change. The first person must guess the nature of the change. Repeat, with the other partner making the change.

3. Ask the class to close their eyes and answer the following questions:
   a. How many doors are there to the entrance of this building?
   b. What color is the floor?
   c. What color socks are you wearing?
   d. How many lights are in the ceiling?
   e. What are the predominant shapes in the room?
   f. How many windows are in the room?

4. Ask the class the following questions:
   a. Is the red light on a traffic signal on the top or bottom?
   b. Is a stop sign hexagonal or octagonal? What color is it?
   c. Does water go down the drain clockwise or counterclockwise?
   d. What color is your mail delivery vehicle?
   e. What is the logo for a Honda? A Toyota?

— Notes —

1. Alane Jordan Starko, *Creativity in the Classroom*, 2nd ed. (Mahwah, NJ: Lawrence Erlbaum Associates, 2001).

2. Howard Gardner, *Frames of Mind* (New York: Basic Books, 1993).

3. Albert Rothenberg, *On Creativity and Madness* (Baltimore, MD: Johns Hopkins University Press, 1990).

4. Jerome Bruner, *On Knowing* (Cambridge and London: Belknap Press, 1979).

5. Robert and Michele Root-Bernstein, *Sparks of Genius* (New York: Houghton Mifflin, 1999).

6. Emily T. Smith, "Are You Creative?" *Business Week* (Sept. 30, 1985).

7. Robert Friedel, "The Accidental Inventor," *Discover Magazine* (October 1966).

8. Michael LeBoeuf, *Imagineering* (New York: McGraw Hill, 1980).

9. Stephen Jay Gould, "Creating the Creators," *Discover Magazine* (October 1996).

10. LeBoeuf, *Imagineering*.

11. Jean Piaget, *Plays, Dreams and Imitation in Childhood* (New York: W. W. Norton, 1951).

12. Viola Spolin, *Theatre Games for the Classroom* (Evanston, IL: Northwestern University Press, 1984).

13. *The Puppet Book,* 2nd ed. Edited by L. V. Wall, Ga. A. White & A. R. Philpott (London: Faber and Faber Ltd, 1965). The Educational Puppetry Association, 232 Southampton Place, London, W. C. I.

14. Root-Bernstein, *Sparks of Genius*.

15. Edward deBono, *Lateral Thinking* (New York: Perennial Library, Harper & Row, 1970).

16. Tom Peters, *The Pursuit of Wow* (New York: Vintage Books, 1994).

17. Hiam Ginott, *Between Teacher and Child* (New York: Avon Books, 1969).

18. E. McIlveen, *Cotton Candy Chatterbox: Verbal Snapshots of Childhood* (Vancouver: Credo, 1990).

19. Joyce Boorman, "She Just Pulled the Blanket Over Her Face," *Early Childhood Creative Arts* Proceedings of the International Early Childhood Creative Arts Conference, Lynnette Y. Overby, (Sr. Editor) Ann Richardson and Lillian S. Hasko (Asst. Eds), Luke Kahlich (Managing Editor), (Reston, VA: National Dance Association [American Alliance for Health, Physical Education, Recreation and Dance]: 2000).

— FOR FURTHER READING —

Balke, E. *Play and the Arts*. Wheaton, MD: Childhood Education, 1997.

Burns, Marilyn. *The Book of Think*. Covela, CA: Yolla Bolly Press, 1976.

Chaille, C., and S. Silvern. *Understanding Through Play*. Wheaton, MD: Childhood Education, 1997.

Csikszentmihalyi, Mihaly. *Creativity*. New York: HarperCollins, 1997.

Demille, R. *Put Your Mother on the Ceiling* (Imagination games). Santa Barbara, CA: Santa Barbara Press, 1981.

Gardner, Howard. *Creating Minds: An Anatomy of Creativity*. New York: Basic Books, 1993.

Goleman, Daniel; Kaufman, Paul; and Ray, Michael. *The Creative Spirit*. Plume, New York: Penguin Group, 1993.

Hall, Doug. *Jump Start Your Brain*. New York: Warner Books, 1993.

Herrman, N. "The Creative Brain." *Journal of Creative Behavior*, 1991.

Lowenfeld, V., and Brittain, W. *Creative and Mental Growth*, 8th ed. New York: Macmillan, 1987.

Marks-Tarlow, T. *Creativity Inside Out: Learning through Multiple Intelligences*. Reading, MA: Addison-Wesley, 1995.

Parnes, Sidney. *Creative Behavior Guidebook*. New York: Charles Scribner & Sons, 1967.

Rogers, E. "Toward a Theory of Creativity." In *A Source Book for Creative Thinking*, edited by S. J. Park and H. F. Harding. New York: Scribners, 1983.

Sark. *A Creative Companion*. Berkeley, CA: Celestial Arts, 1991.

Stout, C. J. *The Art of Empathy: Teaching Children to Care*. Blauvelt, NY: Art Education, 1999.

Torrance, E. P. *The Importance of Falling in Love with Something*. Cincinnati, OH: Creative Child and Adult Quarterly, 1983.

Von Oech, Roger. *A Whack on the Side of the Head*. New York: Warner Books, 1983.

———. *A Kick in the Seat of the Pants*. New York: Warner Books, 1986.

———. *Creative Whack Pack*. Stamford, CT: U.S. Games Systems Inc., 1992.

Wolpert, Louis, and Richards, Allison. *Passionate Minds*. Oxford University Press, 1997.

PART II

The Art Forms

What Students Should Know and Be Able to Do in the Arts[1]

There are many routes to competence in the arts disciplines. Students may work in different arts at different times. Their study may take a variety of approaches. Their abilities may develop at different rates. Competence means the ability to use an array of knowledge and skills. Terms often used to describe these include *creation, performance, production, history, culture, perception, analysis, criticism, aesthetics, technology*, and *appreciation*. Competence means capabilities with these elements themselves and an understanding of their interdependence; it also means the ability to combine the content, perspectives, and techniques associated with the various elements to achieve specific artistic and analytical goals. Students work toward comprehensive competence from the very beginning, preparing in the lower grades for deeper and more rigorous work each succeeding year. As a result, the job of experiencing the arts is enriched and matured by the discipline of learning and the pride of accomplishment. Essentially, the National Standards ask that students should know and be able to do the following by the time they have completed secondary school:

- They should be able to communicate at a basic level in the four arts disciplines—dance, music, theater and the visual arts. This includes knowledge and skills in the use of the basic vocabularies, materials, tools, techniques, and intellectual methods of each arts discipline.

- They should be able to communicate proficiently in at least one art form, including the ability to define and solve artistic problems with insight, reason, and technical proficiency.
- They should be able to develop and present basic analysis of works of art from structural, historical, and cultural perspectives, and from combinations of those perspectives. This includes the ability to understand and evaluate work in the various arts disciplines.
- They should have an informed acquaintance with exemplary works of art from a variety of cultures and historical periods, and a basic understanding of historical development in the arts disciplines, across the arts as a whole, and within cultures.
- They should be able to relate various types of arts knowledge and skills within and across the arts disciplines. This includes mixing and matching competencies and understanding in art-making, history and culture, and analysis in any arts-related project.

As a result of developing these capabilities, students can arrive at their own knowledge, beliefs, and values for making personal and artistic decisions. In other terms, they can arrive at a broad-based, well-grounded understanding of the nature, value, and meaning of the arts as a part of their own humanity.

— NOTES —

1. From *National Standards for Arts Education*, published by Music Educators National Conference (MENC). Copyright © 1994 by MENC. Used by permission. The complete National Arts Standards and additional materials relating to the Standards are available from MENC—The National Association for Music Education, 1806 Robert Fulton Drive, Reston, VA 20191 (telephone 800-336-3768).

CHAPTER

3

Art

> . . . it is art that makes us more aware of the human condition . . . its destiny and progress.[1]

James O'Brien

Like music, art is often referred to as the "universal language," for it speaks to us from everywhere. Recording events, social conditions, changing values and more, art provides us with a panoramic view of ourselves—in effect, all our themes and variations as human beings.

The term *art*, as commonly used, has come to embrace a variety of creations—painting, drawing, sculpture, architecture, photography, film, folk art, and many other forms of skillful manipulation and expression. In all of these endeavors we may safely surmise that elements and principles of art played significant roles.

Elements of Art

Elements of art include line, space, shape, form, color, texture, and others.

Painter Paul Klee called **line** a "dot out for a walk." Wherever it goes, line serves artists in many ways—creating a feeling of distance, depth, and **perspective**; delineating contour; directing a viewer's eye to the focal point of a composition; showing paths of movement; simulating texture; and even creating different kinds of feelings.

Horizontal lines, for example, can produce a feeling of tranquility, vertical lines strength and vitality, broken lines violent sensations, and curved lines softness.

Lines are considered connecting points in **space**. When lines enclose space, a **shape** is formed. Such shapes may be the familiar triangle, circle, square, and other geometric figures or simply free forms that do not fall in any special category. Space that is unoccupied in any artwork is known as "negative" or "open" space; the occupied part is termed "positive" or "solid" space. Both are carefully planned because they are equally important.

A shape that is flat, such as the aforementioned geometric figures, is termed two-dimensional. In contrast, shapes that contain depth are classed as three-dimensional and are known as **forms**. These include the pyramid, sphere, cube, cylinder, and cone. (Also classified as a form in art is architecture or the type of sculpture that one may walk around.)

An artist can create the illusion of three dimensionality by darkening one side of a two-dimensional shape and lightening the other. The result is that the viewer sees the object as a three-dimensional form when, in fact, it is simply a two-dimensional shape. This technique is referred to as **trompe l'oeil**, meaning "to fool the eye."

Texture in art refers to the appearance or feel of the surface of the work—rough, smooth, or in between. Certain techniques permit objects to appear rough, for example, when in reality they are smooth when touched by the viewer. When artists use the impasto technique involving the application of several thicknesses of paint, they can create actual texture that may be felt.

For many viewers, **color** is the element noticed first in an artwork. The **color wheel** in Figure 3.1 provides a graphic illustration of colors and their relationships.

FIGURE 3.1
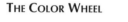

THE COLOR WHEEL

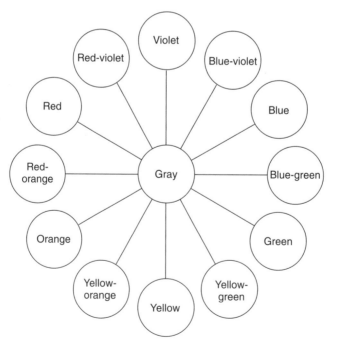

Colors are commonly classified as:

- **Primary:** red, blue, yellow
- **Secondary:** made by mixing primary colors as shown:

green—blue and yellow
orange—red and yellow
violet—red and blue

Complementary colors are those that face each other on the color wheel.

Tertiary colors result from mixing a primary color and a secondary color next to it on the color wheel. These include yellow-green, blue-green, blue-violet, red-violet, red-orange, and yellow-orange.

Warm (or advancing) **colors** contain only reds and yellows; **cool** (or receding) **colors** contain only greens and blues.

The **value** (dark or light) may be changed by adding black to produce a **shade** or adding color to white to produce a **tint**.

Monochromatic is the term applied to a painting in which the artist uses only one color and its derivations.

Changing light may affect the appearance of color. For example, under fluorescent lights, red appears purple or black and under red light green looks black.

MORE ABOUT COLOR

Historically, colors have acquired special meanings in various cultures. For example, purple was identified with power by the Romans and its use reserved for the emperor. Blue was thought to help ward off evil in Islamic countries and often used in decorating walls of their homes. The relationship between red and black was stressed by the traditional Chinese who associated these two colors with the two major parts of the country—north and south—and with other aspects of life. In tomb paintings, colors symbolically protected the dead. In ancient Greece, certain colors represented certain gods—for example, yellow for Athena.

Folklore is full of references to rainbows and the special fascination they have held for various people the world over.

Color in our lives today may relate to comfort, productivity in business as well as health and safety. In everyday living it becomes a consideration in such diverse areas as food preparation, store displays, camouflage, schools, hospitals, and more. Color coding can help locate files in doctors' offices and teach beginners to play selected instruments.

In medicine, dyes are used to stain certain tissues to aid in diagnosing illnesses. Ultraviolet light can produce health-giving vitamin D as well as kill germs. In *Living with Art*, authors Gilbert and McCarter report on a California detention center where violent children were placed in an 8-by-4-foot cell painted "bubble gum pink." Within ten minutes the children "relaxed, became calmer and often fell asleep . . . ." The report further states that in some hospitals premature babies born with jaundice are bathed in blue light to eliminate the need for transfusion. Blue also has been found to lower blood pressure as well as pulse and respiration rate.[2]

Factory owners use color not only to enhance working conditions but also to promote safety. Such color identifications include:

- blue—caution signal
- purple target on yellow—radioactive materials
- orange—acute hazard likely to cut, crush, burn, or shock

Police wear brilliant raincoats to make themselves more visible. Schools and offices use colors that cut down on eyestrain and fatigue. Nature bestows her own kind of protection through the use of colors that provide appropriate camouflage for birds, animals, and other creatures.

Color has been embraced by the agricultural community as well. Based on studies by professor Michael Orzolek, director of the Center for Plasticulture at Penn State, certain plants appear to respond to specific colors, for example, tomatoes grown on a field covered with blazing red plastic doubled their yield. Squash prefer beds of bright blues—not black plastic; cantaloupes and other melons appear to like silvers.[3]

In addition to affecting a wide range of psychological and physiological responses, color is frequently associated with emotional symbolism (red with anger) as well as personality types (black-hearted villain). In early Western films good and evil characters were always distinguishable by the color of their hats.

From a medical college in Wisconsin Maureen Neitz reports that "everyone sees a different palette. . . . That's why people argue about adjusting the color on the TV set." Brain damage may cause some to see the world in shades of gray.[4]

A college student with impaired vision writes, "Color helps me see. With poor vision I've had to learn to make adjustments. I learned to see details through color. It's easier to recognize color than line. I may not see all the leaves on a tree, but I can visualize the leaves by the variations of greens found in nature."

According to Gilbert and McCarter, "The mechanism involved in all these color responses is still unclear, but there is no doubt that color 'works' on the human brain and body in powerful ways."

In summary, color plays many roles in our lives. It can protect us, direct us, identify us, or simply just be there for us. As one student declared, "The color of my house is like one big hug."

> Like acrobats on a high trapeze
> The colors pose and bend their knees
> Twist and turn and leap and blend
> Into shapes and feelings without end.*

So writes Mary O'Neill in a front page of her book *Hailstones and Halibut Bones.*[5] From beginning to end, through her insightful poems, we are

---

From "The Colors Live," from Hailstones and Halibut Bones *by Mary O'Neill and Leonard Wesgard, III. Copyright © 1961 by Mary LeDuc O'Neill. Used by permission of Random House Children's Books, a division of Random House, Inc.*

SLIDES FOR ELEMENTS

Line	*Horizontal Tree*—Mondrian
	Fall Plowing—Wood
	The Bath—Cassatt
	Beach at Trouville—Monet (perspective)
	Brooklyn Bridge—Stella
Shape	*Sea Shell*—O'Keeffe
	Starry Night—Van Gogh
	3 Musicians—Picasso
	Weeping Woman—Picasso
	Broadway Boogie Woogie—Mondrian
	Early Sunday Morning—Hopper
	Still Life—Cezanne
	Beasts of the Sea—Matisse
	Great Wave—Hokusai
	American Gothic—Wood
Color	*Mona Lisa*—Rembrandt
	Picking Flowers—Renoir
	Tragedy—Picasso (monochromatic)
	Sorrow of the Kings—Matisse
Texture	*Shoes*—Van Gogh
	Mother and Child—Cassatt
	Madonna and Child—Raphael
	Self Portrait with 2 Pupils—Labille-Guiard, 1785
Forms	*Rocking Chair*—Moore
	The Thinker—Rodin
	Pieta—Michelangelo

---

drawn into a special world of meeting colors in new ways—each one transformed into an entity in itself—and touching our souls in the process.

Elements of art are present in all artworks. The suggestions in the above box are offered here merely as examples of the use of various elements as well as introductions to the work of well-known artists. A few of these may also be used to illustrate principles of art, periods, and styles.

Principles of Art

When all of the available elements are assembled, an artist must then explore certain guidelines for organizing them into a satisfying work of visual art—in much the same way that a composer uses form as a structure for organizing musical elements.

These guidelines are commonly referred to as **principles of design** or simply principles. They include balance, emphasis, rhythm, unity, variety, proportion, and others.

Balance refers to visual weight and may appear as any of the following:

- **Symmetrical** (formal)—both sides of the work are organized as to appear to be equal
- **Asymmetrical** (informal)—one side of the work is unequal to the other
- Radial—the main body of the work appears in the center, with the other parts radiating around it

When considering balance, an artist must be aware that large, dark, textured objects centrally placed will appear heavier than small, light, nontextured objects of the same size placed near the edge of the work.

Emphasis means that the artist has designated parts of the work to which the viewer's eye will be immediately drawn and will manipulate the elements (line, light, color, and others) in certain ways to accomplish this.

Rhythm in art is created through repetition of various elements forming patterns. Types of patterns include repeating (all alike), alternating (one large, one small), or progressive (increasing or diminishing in size). Repeating elements in an art composition can bring **unity** to the work, giving the viewer the feeling that everything seen belongs together.

A touch of **variety** in the form of a different shape, color, and so on will ensure interest in the piece. **Proportion** is mainly concerned with size relationships between objects.

Genres of Art

The word *genre*—meaning category or classification—is commonly heard in connection with all arts.

When referring to visual arts, "genre" may embrace a large category such as painting, architecture, sculpture, and others, as well as a particular species of it. Classifications of painting, for example, may be based on subject matter (still life, landscape, seascape, portrait, etc.), media used (oil, watercolor, etc.), as well as the historical period to which it belongs (**Renaissance**, Classical, Romantic, etc.).

Sculpture is often referenced by the terms bust, full figure, relief, full round, equestrian, kinetic, and others. In addition, certain kinds of sculpture may be grouped according to the processes used to create them (addition, subtraction, manipulation, substitution). Being aware of these techniques can enhance appreciation of this art form and increase the range of opportunities for producing it in the classroom.

Artworks are also frequently classified by style (e.g., **Impressionism, Cubism**, representational abstract, etc.). In the 1960s styles fell under such headings as **pop**, **op** (optical), and "minimal" as artists became interested in contemporary subjects such as comic strips (Lichtenstein), films and commercial products (Warhol), and other reflections of mass-produced culture. Later, the scheme was broadened by Sol Lewitt's "conceptual art"—dealing solely with an idea—and Laurie Anderson's **performance art**—dealing with everything. In between, Christo covered bridges and islands with polyethylene, lined up umbrellas, and made each project disappear almost as quickly as it appeared.

Some traditionalists may not view some of the aforementioned creations as "art"; however, artists have always been among the first rule breakers.

A topic of interest might be to speculate what rules will be broken next, provided we can figure out what the rules are.

For Discussion

1. Consider the following statement carefully, and then comment on what you feel are its implications:

   There is nothing in the arts that is not based on the human experience.

   Isaac Stern

2. Using several different sources, explore the meaning of the word *aesthetic*. What do you think is meant by the "aesthetic experience?"
3. Search out examples of art in public places, and then comment on what you perceive as its purpose in each setting. Aside from bringing us pleasure, what other functions is art serving in our lives?
4. Nature is frequently referred to as a "sculptor." Comment on the examples of this you have observed.
5. Reflect on the following:
   a. What letters of the alphabet are symmetrical? Are there any symmetrical numbers?
   b. If you were folded in half the long way would the result be symmetrical?
   c. What color would you choose for a sigh? a laugh?
   d. What sounds do you hear when you see the color red?
   e. What color do these words evoke when you hear them? trust, greed, hallelujah
   f. If you could paint the wind, what color would it be?
6. Identify settings in present-day living where you have noted color being used in various ways for specific purposes.
7. In what ways do you think color might be used in the future?

Art-Related Activities

The activities suggested below are intended for college students who, in turn, may adapt them for future use in their classrooms, if desired.

1. Go for an exploratory walk to discover examples of the following in the environment:

   a. Elements of art
   b. Symmetry and asymmetry balance
   c. Patterns

2. Divide into several groups. Select an "artist" for each group who will create a human landscape with each group member assuming an identifiable part of the picture (tree, hill, etc.). Consider balance and other principles when planning. Before "freezing" in place for others to view, the artist also assumes his/her position as part of the work.

3. Divide into several groups. Assign each group a primary or secondary color. Have them elicit as many responses as possible to complete the statement, "(Color) is _____." Suggest avoiding common connections (yellow—sun, etc.). Encourage exploring less conventional paths based on observations that will reflect more creative thinking. Have two groups blend together to form a new color and repeat as before.

4. Divide into two groups—A and B. Identify counterparts in each group. Have one person in Group A assume a position, followed by the remaining group members, adding on one at a time to form a human sculpture. Remind group that the finished piece must contain examples of negative and positive space. The chosen places/positions of Group A should be carefully observed by their counterparts in Group B. When complete, Group A melts out and Group B reproduces the sculpture.

5. Repeat as in activity no. 4 above, except create a human **kinetic sculpture** (one with moving parts). When complete, transform into a kinetic *sound* sculpture adding sounds that reflect the type of movement(s) selected.

6. Divide into several groups. Have each group think of as many representations of the word *line* as possible (e.g., lifeline, clothesline, out of line, etc.) and then portray their selection in tableau for other groups to identify.

7. Divide into several groups. Assign each group a shape. Have them represent the shape in as many ways as they can with their bodies, moving or still. Using the same groups, let each group choose a form (sphere, cone, etc.) to represent for others to identify.

Experiencing Art in the Classroom

Every child is an artist; the problem is how to remain an artist once he grows up.

Pablo Picasso

Art, like music, offers many opportunities for self-fulfillment in the classroom because of its broad range of materials and processes that enable children to choose appropriate avenues for communicating their ideas, feelings, thoughts, and views of their world. Exploring art with children helps to remind us that art lives everywhere and we need only to be closer observers to discover and enjoy the art that surrounds us daily.

Refining the senses is a first step in developing creativity, thus when addressing the visual sense, children should be encouraged to examine common things more closely—a leaf, flower petal, multicolored rock, a piece of wood cut to show the grain, and others. In addition, a reminder to look at objects from different angles—underneath, upside down, sideways—can be an early initiation into later problem solving. Experiences in the visual arts can also facilitate coordination between hands and mind, aiding development of psychomotor, affective, and cognitive skills.

As teachers are probably aware, respected arts educators frown on the use of coloring books, not only because they are limiting, but also because experts such as Lowenfeld and Brittain tell us that "more than half of all children exposed to coloring books lose their creativeness and their independence of expression and become rigid and dependent."[6] These authors also maintain that coloring books make children inflexible, fail to provide emotional relief, discipline, or skills, and condition a child to "adult concepts that he cannot produce alone and that, therefore, frustrate his own creative ambitions." Art projects in the classroom need to be limitless and filled with possibilities for tapping into each child's fertile imagination.

In this connection, when planning art activities, teachers are urged to give careful thought to those projects that truly involve self-expression and exploration, as compared to those frequently classed as "busywork" used to buy quiet time.

Eric Jensen suggests that all who work with children should create what he terms a "good pro-arts environment," beginning in early years. This means that they should be provided with, in Jensen's words, "enough *time* to express themselves . . . *safety* to experiment with different media and from the environment, *respect* so that they know their work is important, *interest* so the child wants to continue, and *support* for a wide range of expression. . . ."[7]

When valuing children's art, it is crucial that evaluation not be based on the reality of the subject matter or the way adults view it. When addressing a child's green sky or an animal with too many legs, commenting in artistic terms—using the vocabulary of specific elements or principles, such as color, line, balance, and others—not only avoids the hurt of embarrassment for children, but also helps heighten their aesthetic awareness.

Even very young children can become "aesthetically aware" on their own levels in the presence of artworks by the masters. Using such works in the classroom to illustrate some of the basic art concepts or enhance projects under study provides opportunities for deepening relationships with gifted creators and their creations.

MATERIALS

Materials required for a given project will obviously depend on the nature of the project and the grade level; however, since some materials are basic to many art activities, it is suggested that they be kept on hand at all times when space allows. These include:

construction paper	containers for water
watercolor/drawing paper	brushes in different sizes and
newspapers	types (round, flat, etc.)
butcher paper in rolls	glue
manila paper	rubber cement
matting material	scissors
paper towels	Styrofoam cups
waxed paper	straws
paper plates	plastic wrap
crayons	cellophane
markers	string
pencils	toothpicks
colored pencils	fabric scraps
colored chalk/charcoal	sponges
tempera paints	erasers
watercolor paints	brayer (roller for printing)
water-based ink	and tray
pastels/oil pastels	rolling pin
	Styrofoam trays (see safety tips,
	pp. 54–55)
	palettes, if available

These items have also been found to be useful in various ways: Materials of different textures (e.g., sandpaper, rug samples, etc.)

Additional kinds of paper—tissue paper, wallpaper, wrapping paper, aluminum foil

Recyclables, including:

cardboard—corrugated and plain	soda cans
cardboard tubes	candy wrappers
berry baskets	used inkless ballpoint pens
Popsicle sticks	plastic lids
egg cartons	squeeze bottles (clean thoroughly)
boxes	aluminum pie plates
baskets	paper bags
ceramic jars	found objects

Museum and gallery visits are encouraged whenever possible, preceded by proper preparation, of course, in the form of appropriate behavior and the focus of the visit. Contacting the museum staff ahead of time will enable them to supply whatever help they have available to assure a successful trip.

Introducing children to master artworks may begin with an informal discussion centered on what the children actually perceive in the given piece, followed by determination of some of the art concepts present, an invitation to express their feelings about the work, and finally, their assessment of it.

Art creations contain an abundance of information about the lives and times of those who lived before us; thus, viewing the masters can provide not only aesthetic pleasure but also a basis for discovering connections between art and other disciplines.

In many ways, art can teach us more about history than historians who write of it.

MAKING ART

Classroom teachers who feel at risk when entering the area of art with children should be assured that the numerous project possibilities as well as the easy availability of materials for implementing them will guarantee success in the venture for even the faintest of heart.

The following pages represent mere samples of areas customarily covered in classroom art. In view of limited space and new ideas emerging even as we write, the information is not expected to be the total sum, by any means. For those whose confidence swells in the initiation process, inspiring them to further pursuits, creative ideas abound in publications, sharing colleagues and the Internet. (See For Further Reading.)

It should also be noted that the range of activities may be considerably broadened by simply inviting children to originate new tools and processes as well as explore different ways of using conventional ones. In addition, different venues can spark ideas that transcend the traditional. For example, sculpture beyond clay, paper, and fabric may be created by venturing into the less familiar—a melange of earth, rocks, branches, pine cones, grasses, and other yields of nature, arranged in a selected outdoor setting that becomes transformed into a component of the work.

Finally, where applicable, art experiences may be enriched by "word-scapes" of historical connections, events, tales, myths, and other meaningful enlightenments related to the given project.

Projects

Art elements can provide a rich basis for many varied creations such as those suggested here related simply to line and shape.

Introductions begin with observation—the essence of visual artwork.

1. Increase awareness of line, shape, and contour by observing/studying more closely the varied outlines of such forms as:

    a. Trees (e.g., willow, weeping cherry, Norway spruce, white pine, columnar maple, redwood)

    b. Flowers (e.g., snapdragon, peony, rose [bud and flower], amaryllis, daisy, bird of paradise)

    c. Animals (e.g., giraffe, fox, lion, kangaroo)

    d. Small land creatures (e.g., hummingbird, praying mantis, ladybug, spider)

    e. Sea creatures (e.g., starfish, octopus, whale, sea urchin)

    f. Mountain ranges (e.g., Tetons, Andes, Rockies, White Mountains, Himalayas)

    g. Coastlines of various oceans

    h. Buildings, automobiles

    i. Skylines of different cities

2. Be a "track detective." Study the lines and shapes of tracks made by animals, vehicles, and humans, as well as footgear used in different sports.

3. Draw shapes of symbols that represent special times of the year (St. Patrick's Day, Christmas, Hanukah, Halloween) and then create a "shape" calendar for each month. Invent a new special day and create a symbol to represent it.

4. Create a visual image that represents what "goodbye" means to you. Do the same with "hello."

5. Cut construction paper of one or more colors into small shapes and glue onto another sheet of paper in any arrangement desired. Give the completed piece a title.

6. Using an art tool of choice, draw any shape you feel best represents the way anger feels.

7. Using jar covers or other round objects, trace circles on a piece of paper. (Twelve circles should fill an 8 1/2-by-11-inch size paper.) Create something different out of each circle by drawing or painting on it, or cut out circles and put them together in any way desired. (Student designs have ranged from phases of the moon to circle books and centipedes.)

8. Draw different sizes of the same shape and combine them to create an object; for example, stacked squares can become a robot.

9. Combine geometric shapes to form designs or objects; for example, a rectangle and a circle can make a simple tree, three circles a snowman, and with the addition of a few lines, two ovals can equal a cat.

10. Explore the meaning of "theme and variations" and then select a shape and create as many variations of it as possible.

11. Using an oval for the head, draw stick figures out of lines arranged in ways that reflect different poses modeled by other students.

12. Insert one hand into a bag of different-shaped objects without looking into the bag. Select any of those touched and draw it with the other hand.

13. Study which geometric shapes seem to come closest to resembling those that make up a human figure (e.g., oval—head), and then draw the figure using the shapes selected.

14. Use different art tools to draw (or paint) many different kinds of lines (thick, thin, crooked, etc.) going in various directions. Choose several that you like, and then create a line composition using only those selected.

15. Cut strips of construction paper into line shapes and glue onto contrasting colored paper in any desired arrangement. Give the finished piece a title.

16. Using a squeeze bottle white glue, draw lines of various types onto dark-colored construction paper. Let dry.

17. Draw a line that represents the way peace feels, and then another line expressing a different emotion.

18. Make a **viewfinder** like film directors use to define a scene. Simply fold an index card, and cut the shape of a rectangle or square on the fold. Open to view any desired scene.

19. Using a piece of manila paper approximately 6-by-7 inches in size, fold in half the long way. Cut a design on the fold, open and color the cut edge with a crayon, and then lay on another piece of paper. Transfer the design by rubbing the colored edge with your finger to transfer onto the other paper. Repeat the design by placing elsewhere on the same paper. For variation, reverse the manila paper, use a different color on that edge, and repeat as before.

20. Use line to create perspective:
   a. Measure an inch from the top of a sheet of plain or construction paper and draw a line from the left side to the right all the way across. Mark the center of the line.
   b. Draw a line from the marked center to the left side of the paper, then another line from the center to the right side.
   c. Imagine a scene in this setting (rural, urban, or other). Place the appropriate objects and/or figures in the drawing using color in any form desired.
   d. For variation draw (or paint) objects and/or figures of varying sizes on cut strips of paper of different widths (small figures on narrow strips; large figures on wider strips) and place in perspective.

DRAWING AND PAINTING

Pencil, pen and ink, crayons, oil pastels, markers, colored pencils, and charcoal are tools most commonly associated with drawing. Less conventional implements may be found among twigs, feathers, rubber gloves, corks, soap, and others.

Crayons can produce different effects when used in different ways such as varying the pressure exerted (heavy for a darker result), changing the coloring surface, or a combination of the two (using the wide side to represent an object, then outlining the object with the point). Combining crayons with other art media such as paint, for example, can create interesting results.

Although brushes (and hands in early grades) are the usually accepted tools for painting, unusual effects may be produced with sponges, string, straws, wadded paper towels, combs, eyelash brushes, Q-tips, forks, popcorn, marshmallows, balloons, and assorted size balls used in various ways.

Painting liquids may also invite experimentation. Besides the conventional watercolor, tempera, and acrylics, interesting results can be achieved using berry juices, food dyes, tea, coffee, liquid wax, melted crayons, glue, and other fluids.

Painting and drawing surfaces can range from paper (tissue, crepe, butcher, construction, towels, plates, bags, newsprint) to wood, stone, glass, aluminum foil, cardboard (plain and corrugated), cloth, sand, and more.

Paint may also be applied in different ways for variation.

Projects

1. Select and arrange objects into a still life and draw.

2. Design a new logo for a product or company.

3. Draw around feet, cut out, and arrange in a walking pattern in different directions.

4. Draw outline of body on long roll of butcher paper. Fill in details and clothing.

5. Sit opposite a partner and draw his/her portrait. Draw a self-portrait and compare the likenesses.

6. Experiment with drawing an animal using just one line in the manner of artist Alexander Calder.

7. Experiment with wet and dry brushes as well as those of various widths and thicknesses for producing different effects.

    a. Mix primary colors to create secondary colors. Use a brush (or other tool) to mix or dip one hand in one primary color, the other hand in another, and rub together to form a secondary color.

    b. Make a color wheel showing primary, secondary, and tertiary colors.

8. Apply paint in different ways:

    a. Hold a dripping paintbrush over the paper and move in various directions over the entire surface taking care not to touch the brush to the paper.

    b. Attach a piece of fine mesh (wire or nylon) to a frame. Elevate over paper and paint with toothbrush on mesh to achieve a spatter effect on the surface below. Vary by placing any desired shaped object (e.g., leaf) on paper. When spattering is completed, lift object to view design made.

9. Place paper in a shallow pan or in shoe box. Dip round objects such as marbles or golf balls in paint, place on the paper, and roll gently to produce designs.

10. Dip flowers into paint. Make multiple prints.

11. To create a simple symmetrical design, fold a piece of suitable painting paper in half; unfold and drop a small dip of paint on one half, fold the other half over, press well, and open to view design.

12. Make ghostly figures by using colored chalk dipped in white tempera paint and draw on black paper.

13. Try creating a painting in the Cubist style of Picasso.

14. Create a **mural** depicting an event, story, or other subject of choice.

PRINTING

Prints are produced by carving a design into a surface or by adding raised objects on top of the surface, applying ink or paint, and then pressing paper, fabric, or other material on the wet surface. The most efficient way to apply the printing medium is with a brayer (roller) wet with ink or paint, rolled on the surface two ways—up/down then left/right to ensure good coverage. Other types of rollers such as rolling pins may also be used.

Ink pads in different colors may be purchased or made by saturating a piece of felt with the desired fluid and placing it on a corresponding size piece of foam rubber. A brayer tray or flat plate covered with layers of paper towels work well for paint.

Depending on the grade level and objectives, incising implements may range from an inkless ballpoint pen (for Styrofoam, clay, plaster, etc.) to other more sophisticated cutting/carving tools intended for wood or linoleum blocks.

PRINTING/STAMPING TOOLS

bottle caps	paper towel rolls
drinking glasses	ears of corn
cookie cutters	muffin pans
corks	leaves
plastic alphabet letters	cardboard tubes with cut-out shapes
sponges	buttons of different sizes and shapes
spools	art gum erasers
thimbles	found objects
clothespins	

Note: Some of these objects may require being attached to some sort of a handle or other gripping device to facilitate their use.

Encourage children to experiment with all types of printing tools (p. 49). Whatever tool is chosen, they should be reminded that only the raised surfaces that are covered with the paint or ink will print.

Early printing experiences for young children may begin with handprint and fingerprint designs.

Stamping is done by dipping the tool on the ink pad or in paint and stamping on the desired surface. The list of tools in the Printing/Stamping Tools box is intended to broaden idea bases and to encourage children to find new sources.

SCULPTURE

Although sculpture may appear in different forms and from a variety of materials, clay seems to be the classroom staple from which many delights emerge. It is easy to manipulate, allows for quick changes of mind, can bear much pounding (when venting is in order), and simply feels good to touch. Moreover, it lends itself to a variety of processes such as rolling, cutting, molding, coiling, printing, and decoration and can assume the form of a slab, a sphere, a piece of rope, a puppet, or a beautifully sculpted figure.

Sculptures may also be created from paper, soap, toothpicks, Popsicle sticks, fabric, found materials, ice, sand, and **papier-mâché**.

RUBBINGS

Rubbing is considered everyone's art since it requires no particular artistic talent. The process consists of taping a piece of paper over a carved or textured piece and using the flat side of a rubbing tool, such as a crayon, to rub over the surface, creating a design.

Children enjoy exploring "rubbable" surfaces on which the texture is defined well enough to produce the desired result. Small coins, buttons, embossed book covers, tree bark, gravestones, and countless other objects offer a wide range of possibilities for executing this activity.

It may be of interest to note that the history of medieval, Tudor, and Elizabethan eras was frequently recorded in the form of monumental brass engravings that depicted life of those times—complete with English nobility, armor, heraldry, hair styles, social customs and even pets. Mounted on the walls and floors of parish churches, these memorial plaques sparked great interest in rubbing, attracting thousands of enthusiasts who eventually threatened the plaques' survival. As a result, rubbings of the original brasses are no longer permitted in most English churches.

Fortunately, for those who would still like to pursue this art, the museum of the National Cathedral in Washington, D.C., is headquarters for a rubbing center that offers workshops in which participants are allowed to purchase rag paper (strong and resilient) and nonsmudging beeswax crayons (gold, copper, silver, black) to rub brass engravings housed there.

COLLAGE

A **collage** consists of a collection of various materials attached to a firm surface. Such "attachables" may include paper of all types in various forms (cut, torn, curled, crumpled, or otherwise), magazine matter, fabric scraps, natural bounty (leaves, flowers, seashells), found objects, and numerous other items. It may also include some drawing and painting.

Most collages are based on some kind of theme or subject, for example, children frequently choose sports and other recreational pursuits as subjects for their collages. Other themes may vary widely from simple art elements (shapes, lines, colors, textures) to concepts in other disciplines such as math (numbers, patterns, measures), history (events/figures), science (discoveries/inventions), music/poetry, or even broader based themes such as diversity, transportation, communication, and others. More subtle themes such as an emotion (love) or value (respect) are also possible foundations upon which to build a collage.

An "assemblage" results when three-dimensional objects are arranged either on a mounting surface or in a container that may be deep or shallow.

MASKS

Masks are commonly associated with primitive cultures where they played significant roles from rainmaking to preventing illness. In some tribes and cultures such as those in the South Pacific Melanesian islands, mask making is fundamental to their artistic and spiritual lives. Masks in these cultures are for display only and are rarely worn over the face; however, the belief is that their presence will summon powerful, protective spirits. Author Jamie Shalleck reminds us that masks still exist today in various forms and writes of them from a slightly different perspective in the book *Masks*[8] from which the following is excerpted:

> Masks are familiar social accouterments but very few of us recognize them as such. Perhaps we have not taken the time to look, or perhaps our stereotyped notions are blinding us . . . the masks we recognize most easily are those primitive tribal offerings that hang useless and out of context in our museums . . . spiritless remains of another social mode . . . unrelated to our current needs and interests.
>
> But here and now masks do prevail—masks that we all wear, whether consciously or unwittingly. With a little practice, one can recognize them easily.
>
> By definition, a mask is some alteration of the face—a change of appearance for purposes of protection, make-believe, social acceptance, disguise, amusement or religious devotion. A mask is the spirit realized—inner urges given shape and form and displayed upon the face. A mask is also a medium through which the gods can be invoked. It is an invitation to the gods to inhabit an appropriate and available

form, the mask itself, in order to communicate with the human tribe. A mask can attract or repel, reassure or frighten. . . .

Contemporary mask-makers include companies that manufacture gas masks, women who make themselves up, surgeons who perform cosmetic surgery and political public-relations consultants.

We wear masks every day—when we put on sunglasses . . . cosmetics . . . veils . . . goggles, or peer out at the world through glass windows. Masked and masking, we proceed through life, modifying our appearance to suit the occasion or the drama.

It is interesting to speculate that our curiosity about one another—our desire to meet and understand other social creatures—has something to do with the masks we wear. In fact, this curiosity may be nothing but the wish to discover the rationale for a particular mask, the extent of an individual's mask wardrobe, or the "true" face behind the recognized mask. Because our society is complex and each of us is called upon to play a variety of roles . . . few of us can afford to go about bare-faced. One can argue that we are never maskless; honesty can be a mask.*

Did you know that Charlotte Brontë's father persuaded his children to speak more frankly by giving them each a mask to wear? What mask are you wearing today?

Making Masks

Although masks are frequently made as art projects, they are at home in all the arts—particularly drama where they may serve as springboards for a range of characterizations in varied settings.

The foundation of a mask may be a simple paper bag, paper or plastic plate, or a piece of cardboard cut in an oval shape and scored for easy bending in the middle. More sophisticated creations can be made from clay, plaster, or weaving materials and decorated with feathers, natural, found, and other objects.

Plastic bowls or balloons provide good bases for papier-mâché upon which faces can be painted when dried.

Simple totem poles may be erected from a series of masks drawn or painted on construction paper and wrapped around a pole or stacked ice cream cartons decorated with appropriate symbols.

Mask making may be enriched with explorations into the uses of masks in specific cultures and time periods.

Additional Projects

1. Design a hat that reflects your personality, using various materials such as paper, fabric, natural objects, and others.

2. Make a shoshi screen from waxed paper of desired length, painted with liquid starch and adorned with grass, flower petals, tissue, and other objects placed on the starch. Place a second piece of waxed paper over the arrangement. Press

*From Masks *by Jamie Shallek, copyright © 1973 by Subsistence Press. Used by permission of Viking Penguin, a division of Penguin Putnam, Inc.*

with fingers to keep together as it dries. Cut around the outside area. Frame or punch a hole and hang with yarn so that light showing through enhances the design.

3. Punch holes with paper punch into dark-colored construction paper. Attach tissue paper to dark paper with glue diluted with water. Hang where light can shine through.

4. Construct a diorama of any desired scene (garden, beach, room) using a shoe box or other similar container.

5. Create tube people out of cardboard tubes, putting clay heads on top. Attach small pieces of wet clay to heads with toothpicks for facial features.

6. Make an action book from index cards by drawing a person, animal, creature, or any object in different stages of movement in sequence on each card. Arrange cards in order and flip to create the impression of action. (The principle involved is the same as that used by Disney and other animators.)

7. Trace around a shape such as pentagon, hexagon, and others, and then add the same number of traced shapes around the figure using its sides as common ones. Cut the entire piece around its contour, and then into the center in a question mark pattern, stopping at the corner of one of the common meeting places. Accordion fold and complete with same shape cover of heavier weight paper. Decorate and add ribbon if desired to complete the book.

8. Create a visual image of a memorable event in your life.

9. Design a greeting card for a new holiday or occasion that you originate.

10. Spread glue in any design on paper or other appropriate surface. Sprinkle with sand and shake off.

11. Design a personalized license plate for your state.

12. Try bubble blowing through different objects and note shapes formed by the bubbles.

13. Change the color of white or light-colored living flowers by cutting the stems at an angle and placing in a jar of water to which a few drops of food coloring has been added. Wait a few days to allow the flower color to change.

Art Safety in the Classroom

Some art materials contain substances that may produce harmful effects when inhaled, ingested, or brought in contact with the skin. In order to ensure the health and safety of the children, teachers are urged to read all product labels carefully, maintain good classroom hygiene, and study published reports on the subject to help minimize dangers. Children with allergies, respiratory problems, or other conditions that could put them at greater risk should also be identified so that special precautions may be taken when applicable.

According to the Office of Environmental Health Hazard Assessment, "children are generally less able to tolerate exposure to hazardous substances than are adults because of the children's smaller size, higher metabolic rates and immature organ immune systems." This agency also provided the following avoid/substitute list:

- *Avoid:* Products that may generate an inhalation hazard. For example, clay in dry form, powdered paints, glazes, pigments, wet paste, and aerosols such as spray paints and fixatives.
  Substitute: Wet or liquid nonaerosol products. Dry products should be mixed while young children are not present.
- *Avoid:* Hazardous solvent-based products. For example, rubber cement and its thinner, turpentine and other paint thinners, and solvent-based markers.

ART RECIPES

PAPIER-MÂCHÉ

Equal parts of water and liquid starch. Soak strips of newspaper in liquid. Mix wallpaper paste (wheat paste) with water to form fluid paste. Dip paper.

BUBBLE SOLUTION

3 cups water
1 cup liquid soap—baby bath or baby shampoo
1 T. sugar

Mix well. Use fly swatter, berry basket, or tissue tube.

BUBBLE RECIPE

2 cups water
1 cup dish soap
2 T. corn syrup

Mix together. Use pipe cleaners for blowers.

CORN SYRUP PAINT

Add food coloring to light corn syrup. Mix 1 cup of blue, yellow, and red. Place in paper plate for each child. Allow up to five days to dry.

PLAY DOUGH

Mix in a pan: 2 cups flour
1/2 cup salt
4 T. cream of tartar
Add: 1 1/2 cups of water mixed with 2 T. cooking oil

Cook and stir over medium heat for 5 minutes until a dough ball forms. Cool 5 minutes then knead till smooth. Keep in refrigerator in an airtight bag. Food coloring may be added with the liquid if desired.

Substitute: Water-based glues, paints, and markers.
- *Avoid:* Materials that contain lead or other heavy metals. For example, some paints, glazes, and enamels.
  Substitute: Products that do not contain heavy metals.
- *Avoid:* Cold water dyes or commercial dyes.
  Substitute: Vegetable dyes (onion skins, food dyes).
- *Avoid:* Instant papier-mâché that may contain asbestos fibers or lead or other metals from pigments in colored printing inks.
  Substitute: Papier-mâché made from black-and-white newspaper and library or white paste (or flour and water paste).

In summary:

1. Avoid food in the art center.
2. Enforce thorough hand washing after engaging in any art project.
3. Wipe up any spills immediately.
4. Ensure proper ventilation in the work area.
5. See that children wear protective clothing when called for and that hair, jewelry, and other possible hazards be properly confined.
6. Use only new art supplies; refuse acceptance of any donated ones containing unknown ingredients.
7. Discuss safety procedures with children when required for particular projects.
8. Display classroom safety checklist and check it regularly.
9. Watch for exposed cuts/sores on children's hands and arms.
10. Check limits of use of art materials by children with medical problems (allergies), asthma, and other conditions.
11. Use only nontoxic glues and adhesives.
12. Post the telephone number of the nearest poison center in a prominent place. The following agencies and publications can provide more information on this topic:

Art and Creative Materials Institute
1280 Main Street, 2nd Floor
P.O. Box 479
Hanson, MA 02341
Tel: (617) 293-4100
E-mail: debbief@acminet.org

Don Doyle
Department of Education
Visual and Performing Arts Office
660 J Street, Suite 300
Sacramento, CA 95814
Tel: (916) 324-2829

Office of Environmental Health Hazard Assessment (OEHHA)
California Environmental Protection Agency
Integrated Risk Assessment Section
1001 I Street, P.O. Box 4010
Sacramento, CA 95814
Tel: (916) 324-2829

Safety in the Art Room
Charles Qualley
Davis Publications, Inc. 1986
Worcester, MA

Art Hazards Information Center
Center for Occupational Health
54 Beekman Street
New York, NY 10038
Tel: (212) 227-6220

Additional information on art hazards is also available from the American Lung Association.

— NATIONAL STANDARDS —
GRADES K–8

Content Standards

1. Understanding and applying media, techniques, and processes.
2. Using knowledge of structure and functions.
3. Choosing and evaluating a range of subject matter, symbols, and ideas.
4. Understanding the visual arts in relation to history and cultures.
5. Reflecting upon and assessing the characteristics and merits of their work and the work of others.
6. Making connections between visual arts and other disciplines.

Source: Excerpted from *National Standards for Arts Education*, published by Music Educators National Conference (MENC). Copyright 1994 by MENC. Used by permission. The complete National Arts Standards and additional materials relating to the Standards are available from MENC—The National Association for Music Education, 1806 Robert Fulton Drive, Reston, VA 20191, telephone (800) 336-3768.

Content standards are designed to be achieved through learning the vocabulary of visual arts (elements, principles, styles, periods, genres, and more), discovering ways of expressing feelings, conveying ideas, communicating meaningful information through various art media techniques and processes, with special attention to refining the sensory equipment and perceiving things in different ways. Studying artworks of master artists as well as those of different cultures will also play a significant role, as will the relating of visual arts to other art forms and subject areas in the curriculum. Art safety is expected to play a role at all times.

— GLOSSARY —

Aesthetic: Pertaining to the sense of the beautiful.

Asymmetrical: Referring to an unequal balance of objects in an artwork. Also called "informal" balance as opposed to "formal" (symmetrical) balance.

Balance: Refers to visual weight of the objects in an artwork. Principle of design.

Collage: Artwork made by attaching various objects to a flat (two-dimensional) surface.

Color: Art element. Contains properties of *hue* (named color, e.g., red), *value* (lightness or darkness), and *intensity* (bright or dull).

Color wheel: A circular representation of all color classifications and their relationships.

Cool colors: Related colors predominated by blue, green, and violet.

Complementary colors: Those colors opposite each other on the color wheel.

Cubism: A style of twentieth century art in which artists interpreted subjects in geometric forms, particularly the cube, pyramid, cone, and cylinder. Pablo Picasso is often designated as the "father" of Cubism.

Elements of art: Line, space, shape, color, and texture.

Emphasis: Refers to the use of various artistic devices (e.g., color, shape, etc.) for drawing the eye to particular objects or areas in an artwork. Principle of design.

Form: Three-dimensional shape containing depth, for example, pyramid, sphere, cone, cylinder, and cube. Also the way elements are organized in an artwork.

Genre: Category or classification.

Impressionism: Art style of the late nineteenth and early twentieth century in which artists used short unblended brushstrokes or dashes, bright colors, and natural light to create an "impression."

Kinetic sculpture: Sculpture with parts that move either by air currents or by mechanical means.

Line: A connecting point in space; outline of a shape. An element of art.

Monochromatic: Refers to one color and its derivations.

Mural: Large wall painting applied directly to the wall or on selected material to hang. May be based on a chosen theme, event, or other subject.

Op art: Art style of the 1960s related to creating optical illusions through line, shape, and various patterns.

Papier-mâché: Made from paper pulp or strips of paper mixed with paste, glue, or starch and molded into various shapes. May be painted and decorated when dry.

Performance art: Art genre involving live movement, music, visuals, and more; sometimes involving several individuals along with the artist.

Perspective: Representation of a sense of distance and depth in an artwork through use of line and other elements.

Pop art: Art style of the 1950s and 1960s based on popular culture, for example comics, film stars, brand names of products, and so forth.

Primary colors: Red, blue, and yellow.

Principles of design (or art): Guidelines used by artist to organize art elements in their artworks.

Print: Made by covering a block or other object with paint and transferring the design to a flat surface.

Proportion: Size relationship between objects in an artwork.

Renaissance: The 300-year period of revival of interest in Greek and Roman classical art, philosophy, science, human beings, and their environment. Also called the "age of painting."

Rhythm: Repeated patterns, lines, shapes, colors, and other elements in an artwork. Principle of design.

Rubbing: Made by placing a piece of paper over a textured object and rubbing with a flat-sided crayon or soft pencil to produce a design.

Sculpture: Three-dimensional artwork that may be made from a variety of materials (clay, wood, fiber, etc.) using different processes (carving, modeling, etc.).

Secondary colors: Green, orange, and violet. Made by mixing two of the primary colors (e.g., red + yellow = orange; blue + yellow = green; red + blue = violet).

Shade: Created by adding black to a given color to darken its value.

Shape: Two-dimensional character or form defined by its boundaries (e.g., triangle, square). Element of art.

Space: Open areas between or inside shapes. An element of art.

Symmetrical: Referring to an equal balance of objects in an artwork. Also called "formal" balance as opposed to "informal" (asymmetrical).

Tertiary colors: Made from mixing a primary color and the secondary color next to it on the color wheel (e.g., yellow green, blue green, etc.).

Texture: Refers to the way the surface of an artwork feels or looks. May be actual or simulated, depending on the technique used by the artist.

Tint: Created by adding a given color to white to lighten its value.

Trompe l'oeil: Meaning "to fool the eye," refers to the appearance of volume where none exists.

Unity: Desirable effect achieved when all parts of an artwork seem to belong together. Principle of design.

Value: Relating to lightness or darkness of a color.

Variety: Various types of lines, shapes, and other art elements used in an artwork to heighten interest. Principle of design.

Viewfinder: A small opening cut in paper or cardboard showing what will appear in the film or photograph when completed.

Warm colors: Related colors predominated by reds and yellows.

— NOTES —

1. James O'Brien, "A Path to Understanding and Enjoying the Arts," *Music Educator's Journal* (May 1994).

2. Rita Gilbert and William McCarter, *Living with Art*, 2nd ed. (New York: Alfred A. Knopf, 1988).

3. M. D. Orzolek, and J. H. Murphy, 1993 *"The Effect of Colored Polyethylene Mulch on the Yield of Squash and Pepper,"* Proceedings National Agricultural Plastics Congress (24: 157–161).

4. Sharon Brownlee, with Traci Watson, *Senses* in U.S. News and World Report January 13, 1997.

5. Mary O'Neill, *Hailstones and Halibut Bones* (New York: Doubleday, 1961).

6. V. Lowenfeld and W. L. Brittain *Creative and Mental Growth* (New York: Macmillan, 1987).

7. Eric Jensen, *Arts with the Brain in Mind* (Alexandria, VA: Association for Supervision and Curriculum Development, 2001).

8. From *Masks* by Jamie Shalleck, copyright © 1973 by Subsistence Press. Used by permission of Viking Penguin, a division of Penguin, Putnam Inc.

— FOR FURTHER READING —

Antoine, Veronique. *Picasso: A Day in His Studio* (Art for Children). Broomall, PA: Chelsea House, 1994.

Arons, Linda. *Art Projects Made Easy*. Englewood, CO: Teacher Idea Press, 1995.

Baillet, Yolande. *The Impressionist* (Art for Children). Chelsea House, Sept. 1994.

Brady, Martha, and Gleason, Patsy T. *Artstarts*. Englewood, CO: Teacher Ideas Press, 2000.

Brittain, W. Lambert. *Creativity: Art and the Young Child*. New York: Macmillan, 1991.

Chapman, Laura. *Discover Art*. Worcester, MA: Davis Publications, 1985.

Cressy, Judith. *What Can You Do With a Paper Bag*. San Francisco: Chronicle Books, in association with Metropolitan Museum of Art, 2001.

Gilbert, Rita, and McCarter William. *Living with Arts*, 2nd ed. New York: Alfred A. Knopf, 1988.

Hardiman, G., and Zernick, T. *Art Activities for Children*. Upper Saddle River, NJ: Prentice Hall, 1981.

Hobbs, Jack A., and Rush, Jean C. *Teaching Children Art*. Upper Saddle River, NJ: Prentice Hall, 1997.

Holm, Carolyn. *Everyday Art for Kids: Project to Unleash Creativity*. Mockingbird Press, 1996.

Kohl, Mary Ann F. *Mudworks: Creative Clay, Dough and Modeling Experiences*. Bellingham, WA: Bright Ring Publishing, 1989.

Lowenfeld, V. "On the Importance of Early Art Expression." In *Viktor Lowenfeld Speaks on Art and Creativity*, edited by W. L. Brittain. pp. 20–27. Washington D.C. National Art Education Association, 1968.

Massey, S., and Darst, D. *Learning to Look: A Complete History and Appreciation Program for Grades K–8*. Upper Saddle River, NJ: Prentice Hall, 1992.

Schirrmacher, Robert. *Art and Creative Development for Young Children*. New York: Delmar, 1998.

Schuman, J. M. *Art from Many Hands*. Worcester, MA: Davis Publications, 1981.

Simpson, Judith; Delaney, Jean; et al. *Creating Meaning Through Art*. Columbus, OH: Merrill, Pearson Education, 1998.

Wachowiak, Frank, and Clements, Robert D. *Emphasis Art*, 6th ed. New York: Longman, 1997.

— ART-RELATED RESOURCES —

Slides, prints and other art-related materials are available from a variety of sources such as the following:

Guggenheim Museum
1071 Fifth Ave.
New York, NY 10128
Website: www.Guggenheim.org

University Prints
37 Cottage St.
Sanford, Maine 04073
Website: www.uni-prints.com

Metropolitan Museum of Art
Fifth Ave. at 82nd St.
New York, NY 10028
Website: www.metmuseum.org

Museum of Modern Art
11 West 53rd St.
New York, NY 10019
Website: www.moma.org

National Gallery of Art
2000B South Club Drive
Landow, MD 20785
Website: www.nga.gov

Note: The website www.webmuseum displays an extensive collection of masterworks that may be printed out on any home printer; however, the quality (especially color) of the print may vary depending on the printer.

The following websites may also prove helpful in finding ideas for classroom use:

ArtsEdNe@GETTY.EDU

ArtsEdge, at http://kennedycenter.org

Music

WHEN CHILDREN SING

When children learn to sing,
They rise up strong.
A song will nourish them.
Each tone, each breath
They draw for beauty's sake will feel
The hunger to excel.
And when the world turns cold,
Then music will be bread to warm their souls.[1]

James Heup*

Music is an essential part of human experience, fundamental to human existence. It can soothe, move, inspire, heal, unite, stir us to action, and, as some experts now suggest, even improve our learning capabilities. Music has been a chronicler of history—teaching us about ourselves as we were and are—as well as a reflector of the less familiar lives of others. It would be hard to imagine living without it.

In the education setting, music provides pathways for development in social, cognitive, motor, affective, and creative areas, as well as critical thinking and problem solving. The information shown in Table 4.1 was reprinted from an article by University of Massachusetts professor Roger Rideout in which he expressed his views on various educational theories and their perceived relationship to music pedagogy.[2]

Recent research by University of California (Irvine) psychologist Frances Rauscher and neuroscientist Gordon Shaw has confirmed their earlier studies demonstrating "an unmistakable causal link between music and spatial intelligence"—the kind of thinking required in complex mathematics.

Studies by Don Campbell, Eric Jensen, Howard Gardner, and others have resulted in some thought-provoking reading related to the need for music and other arts in the school curriculum, and in the process, have sounded a clarion call for educators.

*"When Children Sing," by James Heup. Used by permission of James Heup.

TABLE 4.1

PSYCHOLOGICAL THEORIES AND MUSIC PEDAGOGY

Theory	Major Proponents	Major Tenets
Behavioralism	B. F. Skinner, J. David Boyle, Edwin Gordon, Benjamin S. Bloom, David Krathwohl	Education turns the brain into a mind and molds children into socially acceptable adults. Clearly defined behavioral objectives make learning efficient and assessment demonstrable. Children are motivated by external rewards.
Cognitivism	Jean Piaget, Jerome Bruner	The mind of a child develops through enactive, iconic, and symbolic stages. Children are active, independent learners who can make learning decisions on their own. Learning goals should be individualized to correspond to each child's preferences and level of maturity.
Humanism	Carl Rogers, Abraham Maslow	The study of arts develops a child's highest psychological potential, called "self-actualization." Music can be best taught when tailored to the student's level of maturity, attention, and pleasure. Music should be allowed to impact the student's emotional life.
Socio/ Biological Model	Frances Rauscher, Donald G. Campbell	Exposure to certain musics may effect physical changes in the brain that enhance learning. Including a musical component can augment the study of other core curriculum subjects.

Rideout, Roger. "Psychology and Music Education Since 1950," p. 35 from Music Educators Journal, *September 2002. Copyright © 2002 by MENC: The National Association for Music Education. Reprinted with permission.*

Subtitled "Tapping the Power of Music to Heal the Body, Strengthen the Mind and Unlock the Creative Spirit," Don Campbell's book, *The Mozart Effect*, reveals how music can mend mind and soul, enhance learning, and improve behavior. (School bus drivers will be happy to learn that music can "lessen inappropriate behavior on the bus.") Campbell also cites studies involving the use of rhythm as a tool for developing memory and intellect, indicating that "information spoken in a rhythm pattern will easily hold to-gether as a unit." (Try rapping those math facts!) He goes on to say that drumming can "activate muscle, breathing, heartbeat and brain wave patterns" and that "ten minutes of drumming every day releases tension, resets the mind and body's inner clock and serves as both a stimulant and a sedative."[3] (Note: Any handy drumlike object will do for this activity, for example, a wastebasket.)

In other areas, music can play a significant role in the alleviation of various problems associated with mentally, emotionally, and physically challenged individuals.

For the deaf whose limitation becomes a barrier to social contact, music provides opportunities to communicate with the world of sound through tactile means, becoming the vehicle for teaching rhythm and other aspects of language development. Many individuals who have lost the power to speak are known to have retained an ability to sing, so they are able to establish a needed relationship with others through joining a group in song.

Clinical studies have shown that music may be used sucessfully in behavior modification as well as in reducing autistic blocking. In addition, music has played a role in promoting spontaneous speech in speech-delayed children, improving language skills and speech patterns among minorities and developing or shaping verbal behavior in the mentally challenged.

Music has also become a useful tool in reducing anxiety and fear among children confined to hospitals for extended periods ot time, stressed by confinement and separation from family.

In summary, music activities enable a broad spectrum of special populations to participate successfully, and to experience attendant feelings of improved self-esteem and inner strength—desirable benefits not only for the challenged but for all.

Elements of Music

Although music is made up of many ingredients, the following are generally accepted as its basic **elements**: *melody, rhythm, harmony,* and *form.*

Melody, by one definition "a meaningful succession of tones," by another, "an organized series of tones," is also known by the terms *theme* or *subject*, which can play a major role in certain musical works. When executed singly, each of a melody's tones is characterized by **pitch** (high/low), *intensity* (loud/soft), *duration* (long/short), and **timbre** (pronounced *tam-bre*). Timbre refers to *quality* of the **tone**,—that which makes it distincitive. This quality, in turn, is dependent upon the source of the sound, whether voice or instrument. For example, a tone played on a clarinet will have a very different timbre from the same tone played on a violin or trumpet. Composers and arrangers of large symphonic works select instruments of varied timbres to create the "tone colors" that produce particular effects desired in much the same way that artists choose colors from a painting palette.

Rhythm is a term common to all arts. In music it refers to the basic pulse of the piece as well as to the combination of long and short sounds and silences that ride over the pulse. Sound in music is represented by various kinds of notes; silence by corresponding **rests**—both of which have designated time values. (See p. 106.) In music, silence is as important as sound.

A simultaneous sounding of two or more tones produces a **chord**. When a piece of music contains chords produced either vocally or instrumentally, or when two or more compatible themes are interwoven in the piece, it is said to have **harmony**. The way harmony is manipulated frequently plays a part in determining the **texture** of the music.

The term *form* may have different meanings in music. In one context, form may refer to a specific "genre" or large classification of musical works (**symphony, concerto**, sonata, oratorio, opera, operetta, and others). These large works are divided into *movements* within which there may be a particular type of musical structure also called *form*. The titles of these "small forms" (**canon, fugue**, theme and variations, ABA, and others) represent ways in which the musical content is arranged. For example, a section of thematic musical material *A*, followed by a *contrasting* section *B*, followed in turn by a *repeat* of the original *A* is known as **ternary** (three-part) form and is designated ABA. **Binary** (two-part) form is designated AB and contains a musical idea (theme) followed by a contrasting one (B), but does not repeat the A section as in the ternary form.

Rondo form, represented by the letters ABACA, states a well-defined theme (A) at the outset, which then alternates with contrasting themes (B and C) and returns to A to conclude the piece.

Theme and variations or simply **variations** refers to a theme (melody) that undergoes a series of alterations in the course of the musical piece. These changes may be stated in various ways, for example, **meter** (**duple** to **triple**), melody (ornamentation), **mode** (major to minor), and instrumentation (strings to brass and others).

Free forms, bearing such titles as "rhapsody," "nocturne," and others do not fall into the categories described above; rather, they have their own principles of organization.

Experiencing Music in the Classroom

I hear I forget
I see I remember
I do I understand

Chinese Proverb

The word *music* encompasses a broad range of activities in the classroom—singing, playing instruments, moving, listening, and creating—something for everyone.

Through these varied avenues, children may be afforded the opportunity to explore the world of music through its sound, literature, and language—moving to it, being moved by it, and finally, translating what they have experienced into musical creations of their own. With so many varied activities from which to choose, it is expected that every child will achieve success in some form of musical expression. Our responsibility as educators is to see that all the offerings are there for the choosing.

Although it is agreed that music, as a discipline, possesses its own intrinsic value and designated learning objectives, its presence presents many opportunities for achieving other classroom goals as well. For example, the presentation of certain concepts, such as up/down, soft/loud, fast/slow, and others, can be reenforced when applied in a musical setting. Playing and singing in groups requires a sense of individual responsibility as well as cooperation.

Learning the songs or dances and the vital part that music plays in the lives of cultures other than their own can arouse in children a deeper sensitivity and greater appreciation for diversity.

Finally, participating in some musical activity during the school day offers opportunity for relaxation and needed refreshment.

As previously noted, strong sensory awareness is one of the traits of a creative person. Hearing is one of the senses. Sound is the heart of music; thus, exploring sound seems an appropriate way to begin the joy of sharing music and, in the process, increase awareness, improve concentration, and sharpen listening skills.

EXPLORING SOUND

Vocal sounds refer to those uttered or sung by humans and creatures of land, sea, and air. Although creatures may be somewhat limited in their abilities to make different sounds, human beings have multiple choices. We can talk, sing, whisper, yell, whistle, hum, click our tongues, create popping noises, and perform many other vocal variations.

Body sounds are those made by using different parts of the body in various ways (e.g., stamping feet, clapping hands, snapping fingers, slapping thighs, etc.).

Environmental sounds may be either naturally produced (e.g., surf, wind, thunder, rain, etc.) or other (engines, sirens, appliances, etc.).

Among the universally recognized man-made sounds are those produced by musical instruments—traditional and nontraditional. The latter includes those we make ourselves, as well as other objects we "play" simply because we like the sounds they produce.

To deepen our knowledge of other cultures under study, we need only listen to the sounds of their children's games, street noises, vendor's chants, lullabies, work songs, and other audible expressions of their lives.

Sound Activities

The activities listed below represent some of the ways in which sound may be explored with children.

1. Record a series of frequently heard sounds gathered from different environments—natural and other. Play for children to identify.

2. a. Explore the sound-making possibilities of objects in the immediate classroom environment, at home, on the playground, and in other environments.

  b. Using only one piece of paper try manipulating it in various ways to produce different sounds.

3. Take a sound walk and note all the different sounds heard. Try to classify them as to whether they are natural/other, loud/soft, high/low, pleasing/nonpleasing.

4. Reproduce a range of different human vocal sounds, and then try reproducing some environmental sounds such as the wind, cars passing, and others using the voice only.

5. Explore and imitate vocal sounds made by various animals, insects, and other creatures, for example, frogs, bees, large and small dogs, farm animals, zoo animals, and others.

6. a. Find different ways of clapping (e.g., flat hands, cupped hands, fingers only). Clap with elbows, knees, ankles, and soles of the feet.

  b. Discover other variations of sounds made with the hands and feet (e.g., stamp, tiptoe, shuffle, rub hands together, etc.).

7. a. Imagine what kind of voice a given inanimate object might have, for example, if a tree could talk, what kind of a voice might it use? Select a particular tree and speak in the way you feel it would sound.

  b. Create a dialogue between a tree of choice and a creature that might be living in it or merely climbing on it. Experiment with different sounding voices for each.

8. Reproduce the sound of a *rainstorm* using vocal and body sounds only. Initiate each of the following movements one at a time, cueing each child to imitate. Each movement continues until all are engaged, then the next movement is added. Order of movements:

  a. Brush palms of hands together
  b. Snap fingers
  c. Pat knees
  d. Stamp feet
  e. Add one or two claps for lightning.

When all are stamping feet, reverse the order in the same manner.

9. Form groups. Pass out a card to each group containing the name of a particular sound environment (city street, farm, zoo, etc.). Allow a brief planning time, and then have each group reproduce its assigned sound environment—using vocal sounds only—for others to identify. For a second round, suggest that each group originate a different environment for other groups to identify.

10. Read some "sound poems," making the appropriate sounds vocally as they appear in the text. (See pp. 67–69.)

11. Sing songs containing sounds to reproduce for example, "Comin' Round the Mountain," (train whistle), "Old MacDonald" (animal sounds), "The Bus" (horn), and others.

12. Create some original sound stories, choosing a different sound to represent each character. These sounds may be assigned to various groups who will make the sound each time their character is mentioned in the story. Sounds may be vocal, body, or instrumental—whatever seems most appropriate for each of the characters.

13. Form groups. Have each group create a sound composition using only vocal and body sounds. Suggest that each sound piece should contain some repeating sounds as well as some contrasting ones, and that the beginning, middle, and end are well defined. Allow planning time for these creations.

14. Make some sound-producing instruments. (See "Making Instruments," pp. 85–86.)

15. Explore the sounds and uses of rhythm instruments. (See pp. 82–83.)

16. Get acquainted with instruments of the orchestra. (See pp. 93–97.)

17. Choose any sound desired and do the following with it:

    a. Draw or paint a picture of it.
    b. Write a poem about it.
    c. Build a story around it.
    d. Dramatize it.
    e. Move to it.

SOUND POEMS

Executing the sounds as they appear in the following sound poems[4] will provide opportunities for children to experience a variety of vocal tone colors.

EXCERPTED FROM ONLY THE MOON AND ME

My stomach growls
My throat gurgles
My teeth click
My fingers crack
My toes thump
My nose sniffs
My lips pop

Even my blinks make a sound
I'm really very noisy
In a quiet way.

              Richard Margolis*

EARS HEAR

Flies buzz
Motors roar
Kettles hiss
People snore
Dogs bark
Birds cheep
Autos honk: Beep! Beep!

Winds sigh
Shoes squeak
Trucks honk
Floors creak
Whistles toot
Bells clang
Doors slam: Bang! Bang!

Kids shout
Clocks ding
Babies cry
Phones ring
Balls bounce
Spoons drop
People scream: Stop! Stop!

Lucia/James L. Hymes, Jr.**

I LIKE WEATHER

I like to lie
with sky in my face,
listening to Weather
every place.

Weather is full
of the nicest sounds:
it sings

*"Only the Moon and Me" by Richard J. Margolis. Copyright © 1969 by Richard Margolis. Used by permission of HarperCollins Publishers.

**"Ears Hear" from Oodles of Noodles, © 1964 Lucia and James Hymes, Jr. Reprinted by permission of Pearson Education, Inc.

and rustles
and pings
and pounds
and hums
and tinkles
and strums
and twangs
and whishes
and sprinkles
and splishes
and bangs
and mumbles
and grumbles
and rumbles
and flashes
and CRASHES.

I wonder
if thunder
frightens a bee,
a mouse in her house,
a bird in a tree
a bear
or a hare
or a fish in the sea?
Not me!

I like weather . . .
I don't care whether
it's quiet or noisy
or both together!

      Aileen Fisher*

THE HOUSE CAT

The house cat sits (whispered)
And smiles and sings (on the word "smiles" make a swooping sound)
                (on the word "sings" swoop down and get louder)
He knows a lot (on the word "lot" cup hand, alternately cover and uncover the
mouth several times while sustaining the vowel sound)
Of secret things (repeat word "things" many times, slowing fading out)

      Annette Wynne

Singing

Sharing songs with children can be a most pleasurable pursuit. Any teacher who has missed this joy because of "misperceptions" about personal singing ability is urged to be of strong heart and consider the rewards.

A single song can become the springboard not only for further musical pursuits, but also for those related to other classroom disciplines. For example, the familiar tune "Are You Sleeping" is adaptable in several languages (Bruder Jacob, Fray Felipe, Frere Jacques), useful in tone-matching games (Where Is Billy), can secure better posture (Sit Up Straighter), facilitate finger play (Where Is Thumbkin), and motivate a listening lesson built on a Mahler symphony that features the tune played in a minor mode. In addition, it could conceivably spark discussion on the need for sufficient sleep and/or the sleep habits of various animals, particularly those who hibernate in winter.

The song "I've Been Working on the Railroad" is not only fun to play with musically, but also can arouse interest in early trains, the laying of the first railroad, and discussion related to possible reasons for the decline of the railroad in America.

A song may also spawn activities in related arts—dramatization, creative movement/dance, visual images (using various art media and interpretations), and others, including composing new verses. In the latter connection, composing new verses to familiar tunes may sound fairly benign as an activity; however, it is well to be prepared for surprises. One music teacher reported a small uprising in connection with the song "Minka." The first verse of this Russian folk song tells of the courting of a maiden by a Cossack soldier called to war and his request that she solemnly promise to wait for him. In verse two he returns from battle, finds the maiden too fat, and rejects her—a deed termed dastardly by the fifth grade whose wrath it provoked. In protest, they composed additional new verses in which the Cossack got what he deserved and the maiden fell into the arms of another who accepted her as she was. (Women's advocates are alive and well!)

TEACHING A SONG

Good sources of help in this area—aside from specialists and colleagues—are the CDs/audiotapes accompanying basic music series containing all of the songs found in the books for each grade level. These present the best quality children's voices to imitate and are well produced in terms of child appeal. (See Resources, pp. 116–118).

A **rote song** is one that is learned through the ear. In addition to the recordings mentioned above, songs may also be taught by having the melody played on a keyboard or other instrument (bells, recorder, etc.) while the children follow the words from the board or chart. Teaching by voice may prove the most efficient way for some since it enables the exercising of more control over the process.

Depending on the length or difficulty of the song, the grade level, and the device used, a song may be taught as a whole or in parts. Whatever method is used, the class should hear the whole song through first; then, if desired, it may be broken down into phrases, having the children listen, then repeat one phrase at a time, then two phrases, and finally singing the whole song. For increasing familiarity, the tune may be whistled, hummed, sounded on a kazoo (or similar object), the rhythm clapped, and solos sung on portions of the piece. Songs that are partly familiar, short, and/or repetitious may need practice only on the unfamiliar parts.

The pleasure of singing may be greatly enhanced by pitching each song in its appropriate key and encouraging children to use their "best" voices. Unaware that most children naturally have high, light voices, some adults tend to pitch songs in keys more comfortable for them but too low for children, resulting in sounds that are at best "unchild-like." In the interest of achieving more "musical" goals in this area, the following suggestions may prove helpful:

- Insist on good posture (feet flat on the floor, back reasonably straight, and eyes facing front). In this connection, Campbell reports on the research of French physician Alfred Tomatis, stating, "Sitting or standing upright with the head, neck and spine erect, allows maximum control over the listening process, and stimulates the brain to full consciousness. . . ." In short, posture can affect hearing.
- Practice proper breathing (from the diaphragm). Breathing plays a major part in phrasing—which is beneficial to reading as well as to music. The following exercise can be helpful in acquiring better breathing habits: Encircle the lowest rib with fingers—thumbs to the back, middle fingers touching in front. Inhale, concentrating on forcing the middle fingers apart in the process. Exhale, returning fingers to position. (With more practice and some luck we may get through the first phrase of "America" without taking a breath.)
- Form words on the front of the mouth. Singing properly can improve speech and diction.
- Encourage light singing—avoiding heavy or harsh. This will enable children to sing higher notes with more ease.

HELPING OUT-OF-TUNE SINGERS

Children sing **out of tune** for many reasons—immaturity, physical disability, emotional block, and others; however, the most common has been identified as lack of concentration. Insisting on complete attention, calling attention to light singing, and encouraging every child to sing represent a good start toward the producing of better sounds by all children. For those who need extra help in attaining "in tune" status, tone-matching games are suggested.

Tone-Matching Games

Tone matching may take several forms—from simple roll calling where children simply sing back their names, to longer responses.

When applicable, they may also be related to other subject areas by passing out objects such as colored paper, numbers, or geometric shapes and posing musical questions requiring individual answers in tune:

Teacher: Who has the _____ (shape, color, number, etc.)?

Child: I have the _____ .

The few songs that follow are included here simply as samples of those that might be used to teach concepts, connect with other subject areas, motivate movement, and/or stimulate creative effort. (See Resources for others.)

The Dinosaur Dance
Words and Music by Ned Ginsburg

Used by permission of Ned Ginsburg. From The Music Connection, Book 2 *© 1995 Silver Burdett/Ginn.*

I've Got That Happy Feeling

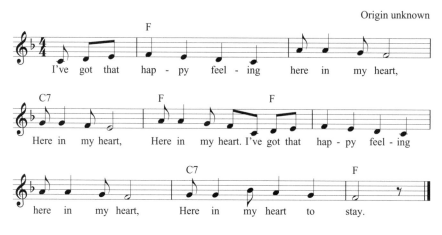

2. I've got that happy feeling down in my feet, *etc.*   *(march in place).*
3. I've got that happy feeling here in my hands, *etc.*   *(clap hands).*
4. I've got that happy feeling all over me, *etc.*

(Have children suggest other verses and actions.)

This Little Light of Mine

2. These little hands of mine, I'm gonna let them clap, *etc.*
3. These little feet of mine, I'm gonna let them tap, *etc.*
4. These little fingers of mine, I'm gonna let them snap, *etc.*

Create new verses.

Two in the Middle

1. Two in the mid-dle and they can't get out.____
   Two in the mid-dle and they can't get out,____
   Two in the mid-dle and they can't get out,____
   Oh, my lil lee. O!

2. Swing you another, and another one in, *etc.*   4. Swing you another, and another one in, *etc.*
3. Three in the middle and they can't get out, *etc.* 5. Four in the middle and they can't get out, *etc.*

When all are in, reverse for subtraction.

From Rhythms Today, *Edna Doll and Mary J. Nelsom © 1965 Silver Burdett Co. Used by permission of Pearson Education Inc.*

Best Friends
Music by Carmino Ravosa

Words by Margaret Jones
Arranged by James Rooker

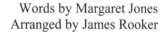

In a relaxed manner

Best friends should be to-geth-er,____ That's how it ought to be,____ So let's pre-tend I'm part of____ you and you are part of me.

Create new verses.

©1971 by Carmino Ravosa and Margaret Jones. Used by permission.

One, Two, Three
Collected by Venoris Cates

1. Head and shoul-ders ba-by, one! two! three! Head and shoul-ders ba-by,

one! two! three! Head and shoul-ders, head and shoul-ders, head and shoul-ders, ba-by,

one! two! three!

2. Shoulders, knees
3. Knees and ankles
4. Ankles, knees
5. Knees and shoulders
6. Shoulders, head

Touch parts of the body as they are mentioned in the song. Clap on "one, two, three."

Che Che Koolay
Singing Game from Ghana

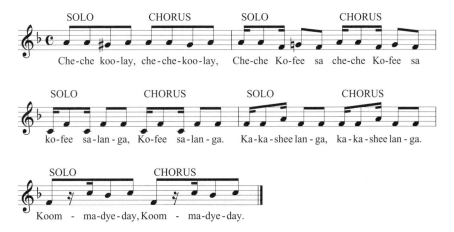

SOLO   CHORUS   SOLO   CHORUS

Che-che koo-lay, che-che-koo-lay,   Che-che Ko-fee sa che-che Ko-fee sa

SOLO   CHORUS   SOLO   CHORUS

ko-fee sa-lan-ga, Ko-fee sa-lan-ga.   Ka-ka-shee lan-ga, ka-ka-shee lan-ga.

SOLO   CHORUS

Koom - ma-dye-day, Koom - ma-dye-day.

From HI. Neighbor (Book 8) By United States for UNICEF United Nations, N.Y.

On Words:	Che-Che Koo-lay	Place: Hands on head
	Che-Che Ko-Feesa	Hands on shoulders
	Ko-Fee Sa-lan-ga	Hands on waist
	Ka-ka-shee lan-ga	Hands on knee
	Koom-ma-dye-day	Bend over & touch toes

Hambone

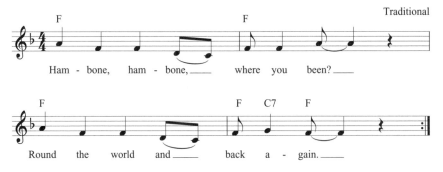

Have children create new verses in reply to teacher's questions, such as:

T: Hambone, hambone, what'd you see?
C: I saw someone just like me
T: Hambone, hambone, what'd you do?
C: I fell down and lost my shoe

New questions may also be suggested by children.

Peace Like a River

2. I ve got joy like a fountain. . .
3. I ve got love like the ocean. . .

"Peace Like a River," words and music from The Music Connection, Grade 3. Copyright © 1995 by Silver Burdett Ginn, Inc. Reprinted by permission of Addison-Wesley Educational Publishers, Inc.

Flowers Won't Grow

Music by Jim Hunter
Words by Tom Paisley

Not too fast

flow-ers won't grow __ And the birds go a-way, __ well, where would we go __ to have

fun and play?

Now that you know, __ I bet you won't throw __

Junk on the ground __ And stuff all a-round. *f* So the birds will play __ And

getting continually softer

flow-ers will grow, __ Flow-ers will grow. __ *mf* Flow-ers will grow. __

Flow-ers will grow. __ *pp* Flow-ers will grow. __ *ppp*

"Flowers Won't Grow," from Silver Burdett Music, Book 3, Teacher's Edition. © 1974 by Silver Burdett Company. Reprinted by permission of Pearson Education, Inc.

Hawaiian Rainbows

Describing a Scene with a dance. Dance directions ←

In Hawaii a beautiful rainbow may appear behind the fleecy white clouds even on a sunny day. People of the Islands use their hands and arms to |tell| about the rainbow.

Children kneel and sit low on their heels. They stretch both arms out to the left, with fingers pointing up and palms facing out.

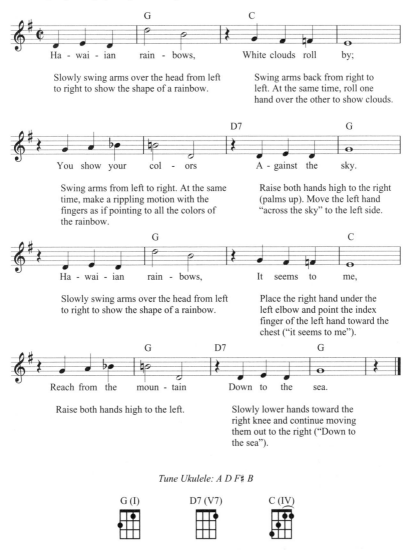

Ha - wai - ian   rain - bows,   White clouds roll   by;

Slowly swing arms over the head from left to right to show the shape of a rainbow.

Swing arms back from right to left. At the same time, roll one hand over the other to show clouds.

You show your   col - ors   A - gainst the   sky.

Swing arms from left to right. At the same time, make a rippling motion with the fingers as if pointing to all the colors of the rainbow.

Raise both hands high to the right (palms up). Move the left hand "across the sky" to the left side.

Ha - wai - ian   rain - bows,   It   seems to   me,

Slowly swing arms over the head from left to right to show the shape of a rainbow.

Place the right hand under the left elbow and point the index finger of the left hand toward the chest ("it seems to me").

Reach from the   moun - tain   Down to   the   sea.

Raise both hands high to the left.

Slowly lower hands toward the right knee and continue moving them out to the right ("Down to the sea").

Tune Ukulele: A D F♯ B

G (I)   D7 (V7)   C (IV)

"*Hawaiin Rainbows," from* Making Music Your Own, . . . © *1968, Silver Burdett Ginn, Inc. Reprinted by permission of Pearson Education. Dance directions from* Growth through Physical Education, *by A.K. Chang, published by Department of Education, Honolulu, Hawaii. Used by permission of Silver Burdett Company.*

SINGING IN HARMONY

Singing in harmony may be initiated in early grades through the introduction of partner songs, rounds, and other simple harmonic devices. These are recommended as beginnings in upper grades as well, when children have had no previous experience with making harmony.

The term *partner songs* refers to two or more songs sung simultaneously, producing an harmonious sound. "Harmonious sound" results only when the songs are pitched in the same key and contain *parallel* chord structures, meaning that the chords designated on the accented beats of each measure in the songs must coincide with each other measure for measure. (Listen to "Pick a Little" sung with "Good Night Ladies" in the Broadway musical *Music Man.*)

The songs listed below may be sung as partner songs. Appropriate keys and starting tones are shown to ensure success:

Song	Key (both songs)	Starting Note
Swing Low Sweet Chariot	F	A (2nd space)
Comin' Round the Mountain		Middle C
Peace Like a River		Middle C
When the Saints Go Marching In	F	F (1st space)
Swing Low Sweet Chariot		A (2nd space)
Are You Sleeping	C	Middle C
Row Row Row Your Boat		Middle C
Three Blind Mice		E (first line)
Farmer in the Dell		Middle C for farmer—Omit The
Skip to My Lou	F	A (second space)
Bow Belinda		F (first space)
Salom Chaverim	d minor	A (below staff)
Hey Ho Nobody Home		D (space below staff)

Basic music series contain songs with harmonizing parts for grades 4 through 8. (See Resources pp. 116–118.) As children move on to upper grade levels they will enjoy singing harmony in two and three parts. In grade 4 children can sing two part harmony carrying two independent parts (soprano and alto); by grade 6 singing may be done in three parts.

Playing Instruments

The term *rhythm instruments* refers to a variety of classroom instruments consisting of sticks, triangles, tambourines, cymbals, drums, jingle bells, finger cymbals, and others. These instruments can be a source of much pleasure to children in all grade levels, as well as valuable learning tools not only in music but also in other subject areas. In this connection, mention should be made of the work of Carl Orff, a German music educator whose method of teaching music to children involves extensive use of various percussion instruments. These include xylophones, metallophones, glockenspiels, tambourines, drums and others—a collection known as "Orff instruments" that may be found in schools where music teachers embrace Orff's theories.

Before engaging in any rhythm instrument activity, the teacher should present each instrument individually, demonstrating how it is to be played to produce its particular sound and calling special attention to the following:

- Ringing instruments (e.g., triangles) must hang free—not clutched in the hand.
- Striking triangles on the inside will prevent them from rotating.
- Cymbals should be passed by each other in a "brushing" motion, not banged together.
- Use crossed position for playing sticks. If one is striated, the other may be run across the striations to make a scraper.

Encourage children to explore different ways of playing the instruments, for example, in addition to shaking and rapping the tambourines, try running the fingers around the jingles or scratching the flat surface gently with fingernails. As familiarity increases, children and teachers will discover new ways of playing as well as new uses for the instruments in other subject areas.

To minimize mishaps and mayhem, it is also helpful to remind children to handle the instruments with care and play only when directed.

Activities

1. Create new words about rhythm instruments to favorite tunes:

   I'll be playing on my cymbals when she comes (Tune: "She'll Be Comin' Round the Mountain")
   You tap your tambourine in (Tune: "Hokey Pokey")
   Old MacDonald had a band (Tune: "Old MacDonald Had a Farm")

2. In songs containing numbers or objects or various counting songs (e.g., "Angel Band," "Twelve Days of Christmas"), sound a different instrument for each number or object each time it occurs in the song.

3. Use rhythm instruments with tone-matching games. (See p. 71).

4. Discover places in various songs where selected rhythm instruments would add interest and/or ethnic flavor.

5. Choose an instrument that best represents the sound of various words, for example, "shiver," "click," and "doom."

6. Heighten dramatic effects in stories and poems with selected rhythm instruments. In this connection, the addition of instruments can also strengthen action (e.g., sticks for fast running) or portray an inanimate object that plays a part (bridge, tree, etc.).

   In stories with many characters, assign a rhythm instrument to each character and play whenever the character appears.

   7. Form groups. Have each group perform a nursery rhyme in sound using rhythm instruments only for others to identify.

   8. Reenforce feeling for meter in music by striking one instrument on the accented beats and a different one on the unaccented beats of selected musical pieces.

   9. a. Show a brilliant or pastel color. Sound each of three selected instruments in turn. Ask which instrument best describes the color.
      b. Repeat with a design.
      c. View a scene in a selected artwork, and then select instruments that best describe it.

   10. Use rhythm instruments with body movement. (See pp. 82–83.)

   11. Use rhythm instruments with music listening selections, when applicable, to enhance active listening and the learning of various musical concepts, for example, theme and variations by using one instrument for the basic theme and different ones for each of the variations when they appear in the music. Patterns in form may also be demonstrated through the playing of selected instruments(s) when one theme is heard and different instruments for a contrasting one.

   12. Sharpen rhythm reading skills by playing a rhythm instrument orchestration from score:

Try the following simple orchestrations to "Jingle Bells."
(B = bells, Tri = triangle, Tam = tambourine, R = rap, sh = shake,
St = sticks, D = drum, WB = wood block, C = cymbals)
𝄽 = rest

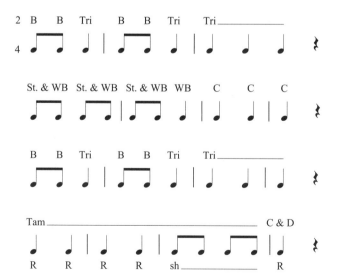

As children gain experience with instruments and an awareness of their qualities, they may create their own percussion scores to musical selections of their choice, basing instrument selections on mood, tempo, rhythm patterns, and other musical considerations.

13. Compose some original rhythm instrument scores to familiar songs or recorded music of choice.

MAKING INSTRUMENTS

If desired, children may make their own simple instruments from various accessible items.

sticks	one-half or one-quarter dowels cut to 12-inch lengths (or shorter for small children if preferred)
triangles	large nail or horseshoe suspended on cord/string

Other ringing instruments may be made from lengths of conduit pipe, bottles, tableware, assorted tools (chisels, etc.), metal disks, pot covers, flower pots of various sizes—suspended from a bar and played with a striker such as a knife, nail, or spoon. Water glasses filled with varying amounts of water may be placed on a flat surface and struck with a metal object as above.

cymbals	pot covers or pie pans (must add holding device)
tambourines	metal disks or flattened bottle caps attached to paper or aluminum plates
drums	large—barrels, nail kegs, large wastebaskets; small—salt and cereal boxes, coffee and shortening cans, ice cream cartons, or other large round plastic containers found in delicatessens. Wooden bowls with rubber or brown paper stretched over the top and laced to secure. Brown paper may be used in place of rubber but must be covered with shellac. Skin may also be available from instrument dealers.

A different kind of drum may be made as follows: Cut four pieces of 1/2-inch thick wood into 12-inch lengths. Attach together to form a square (like a frame), then shrink wrap the whole square tightly. Strike in the center with a hard or soft beater (mallet).

shakers	dried gourds, small dairy cartons, small boxes, fruit juice cans, paper plates taped or laced together, paper or plastic cups taped together at the drinking end, and cardboard tubes covered at both ends may all be filled with rice, seeds, dried beans, pebbles, and even coins. Lightbulbs

covered with papier-máché, then struck to break the globe also make satisfactory shakers.

sandblocks   blocks of wood with sandpaper attached on the sides and bottom. (Add holding device to the top.)

If a strumming or plucking type of instrument is desired, it may be made by stretching rubber bands, wire, or nylon cord over a facial tissue box, shoe box, cigar box, or other similar object that will act as a "resonating chamber." Tighter bands will produce higher sounds.

Humming instruments may be made from combs covered with tissue, and blowing instruments made from straws flattened and cut to different lengths, conch shells, and bamboo.

Hollowed out, dried coconut shells struck together on the hollow side make interesting sounds.

Chimes may be made from 1/2-inch conduit pipe cut to various lengths to produce the desired pitches. These must be suspended from a bar, broom handle, or other device and struck with a metal striker.

A xylophone requires only 1/2-inch thick wood cut into different lengths and laid on a wooden frame. Shorter pieces produce a higher pitch.

Lots of pleasure may be derived from a washtub bass made from a washtub, stick, cord, and a minimum of hardware (see Figure 4.1):

1. With the pail or tub in an upside-down position, drill a 1-inch center hole in the bottom.

2. Place a washer against the hole and insert a 1-inch ringbolt through the hole. Place another washer over the inside hole and add a nut on the end. Tighten the nut to secure the bolt.

3. Drill a hole about 2 inches from the top of a 4-foot stick (broom, mop handle, or dowel) and insert a length of nylon cord or lightweight clothesline.

4. Notch the bottom of the stick to enable it to fit over the bottom rim of the pail.

5. Secure the bottom end of the string to a 1-inch ringbolt and knot the upper end through the hole in the stick. The cord should be tight enough to hold the stick upright.

6. Insert a block of wood under the edge of the pail or tub for better sound.

To play, hold the stick while plucking the cord. Different tones may be produced by pulling back on the stick to tighten the cord.

FOUND INSTRUMENTS

Found instruments include any object or combination of objects that can produce a sound and that may be found anywhere in likely and unlikely places (garage, cellar, kitchen, junkyard, backyard, etc.). Children are urged to explore the total environment for possible yields.

FIGURE 4.1

WASHTUB BASS

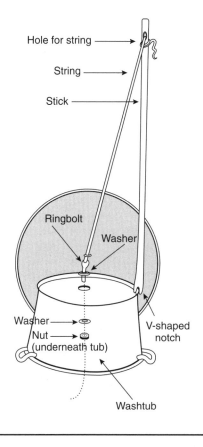

Hole for string

String

Stick

Ringbolt

Washer

Washer

Nut
(underneath tub)

V-shaped
notch

Washtub

Part of the joy of found instruments lies in their exploration and discovery; thus, no lengthy list of possibilities is given here. Past examples have included shampoo and garden hoses to blow and sink drains to strike.

As instruments are brought into the classroom, each child may display the object, tell of its origin, and demonstrate how it is to be sounded. Form groups of instruments with varied timbres and have each group create a sound composition of its own to perform for others. If there is a particular music concept under study such as form, for example, the teacher may choose to use this activity as a way to enhance the learning by suggesting that the compositions be in some designated form such as ABA, rondo, and others. (See p. 64.) Too much freedom can sometimes be intimidating to some individuals when initiating activities such as this; thus, the introduction of a little structure may serve to increase the comfort level.

PLAYING BOTTLES

Bottles may be used to play tunes and chords, providing a source of pleasure in the process. Sound is produced by pressing the bottle against the underside of the lower lip and then blowing gently across the top while at the same time directing the air slightly downward. (A little practice will do it.)

- Select eight soft drink bottles of equal size. Leave the first bottle empty. That will be the designated DO. (Never mind the key.)
- Add water to produce different pitches of the scale tones—DO RE MI FA SOL LA TI DO. The more water added, the higher the resulting pitch.
- When desired notes are in place, line up eight children with low DO to the left and the remaining ascending scale tones in order to the right. At the outset, the teacher may point to each child when it is his/her turn to play. Later, children may play independently through the use of color coding (colored water or construction paper wrapped around bottle) correlated with the color of the written notes, for example, DO—red, RE—green, and so on. If preferred, assign each bottle a number (e.g., DO—1, RE—2, etc.) and play from written numbers.

When children wish to play a piece containing notes lower than the lowest DO, a larger bottle will be necessary. Larger bottles produce lower sounds. (Note: Tuning several bottles to each pitch will enable the entire class to participate.)

Try the following songs shown here with syllables and numbers. Adapt to colors as desired:

TWINKLE, TWINKLE, LITTLE STAR

1	1	5	5	6	6	5	4	4	3	3	2	2	1
DO	DO	SOL	SOL	LA	LA	SOL	FA	FA	MI	MI	RE	RE	DO
5	5	4	4	3	3	2	5	5	4	4	3	3	2
SOL	SOL	FA	FA	MI	MI	RE	SOL	SOL	FA	FA	MI	MI	RE
1	1	5	5	6	6	5	4	4	3	3	2	2	1
DO	DO	SOL	SOL	LA	LA	SOL	FA	FA	MI	MI	RE	RE	DO

ON TOP OF OLD SMOKEY

1	1	3	5	8	6	6	4	5	6	5	
DO	DO	MI	SOL	DO	LA	LA	FA	SOL	LA	SOL	
5	1	3	5	5	2	2	3	4	3	2	1
SOL	DO	MI	SOL	SOL	RE	RE	MI	FA	MI	RE	DO

Chords result from sounding several pitches simultaneously:

DO	MI	SOL	(1	3	5)		
FA	LA	DO	(4	6	8)		
SOL	TI	RE	FA	(5	7	2	4)

and may be used to provide accompaniment for melodies produced by voice, instrument, or other bottles.

Harmonica

Called by many names in its lifetime (French harp, pocket piano, accordion with soul, Mississippi saxophone), this small instrument traces its ancestry far back to the Jew's harp (jaw harp) and the Chinese *sheng*. At one time the harmonica was considered *the* musical instrument of the United States, serving the needs of the lowly and the mighty—from cowboys to presidents.

In his senatorial campaign against Stephen Douglas, Lincoln is reported to have waved his harmonica at the crowd, calling it the "poor man's equivalent" of Douglas's brass band. Presidents Coolidge, Wilson, and Eisenhower all played the harmonica, as did astronaut Wally Schirra who sneaked a tiny version aboard Gemini VI and rattled Mission Control by performing the first "extraterrestrial concert"—his rendition of "Jingle Bells."[5]

Despite some displacement by the advent of less gentle sounding music makers, the humble harmonica is still very much alive and appreciated in recordings by top artists such as Bruce Springsteen, Stevie Wonder, Billy Joel, and others.

The harmonica is included here because it requires only the ability to breathe in and out to play a recognizable tune in minutes—yielding an immediate sense of satisfaction. In short, children can "play now and learn later."

Moreover, keeping their harmonicas prolongs the enjoyment period since children may play them away from school in any favorite place desired. As a result of this extra time and freedom to experiment, many children have been known to develop some special playing abilities.

Harmonicas are available from most music instrument dealers, many of whom will set a special price for schools when quantities are ordered. Because harmonicas are manufactured in different keys, the desired key must be specified when ordering to permit unison playing in the classroom. The key of C was selected here.

PLAYING

The harmonica is usually held in the left hand, with the end resting against the curve of the hand formed between the thumb and index finger. If desired, the right hand may be cupped around the right end of the harmonica with the fingers extended over those of the left hand.

The numbers from 1 to 10 appear starting left to right over the openings. Each opening can produce two different chords, depending on whether the player breathes in or out. The most commonly used openings are 4, 5, 6, and 7.

When blown in that order they sound the notes DO MI SOL DO. When the breath is drawn in over the same openings, RE FA LA and TI are sounded; thus, a complete scale may be played with just those four openings and the two breathing patterns. When reading numbers, a plain number means to blow the breath out:

4   5   6   7

A circled number means to draw the breath in:

④   ⑤   ⑥   ⑦

The numbers indicated for playing scale tones on the harmonica should not be confused with conventional numbering of the notes of a major scale in which DO is always No. 1, RE 2, MI 3 etc. A major scale on the harmonica in the key of C is played by blowing and drawing the numbers as shown below.

Scale Syllables	DO	RE	MI	FA	SOL	LA	TI	DO
Harmonica Numbers	4	④	5	⑤	6	⑥	⑦	7
Letter Names	C	D	E	F	G	A	B	C

Different combinations of plain and circled numbers can produce different tunes such as "Twinkle, Twinkle, Little Star":

4   4   6   6   ⑥   ⑥   6

⑤   ⑤   5   5   ④   ④   4

Children may need to be reminded that when moving from one number to another, they simply *estimate* the distance, and should not remove the harmonica from the mouth to locate the next note number.

The following songs are considered somewhat familiar, for the most part:

TWINKLE, TWINKLE, LITTLE STAR

4   4   6   6   ⑥   ⑥   6   –   ⑤   ⑤   5   5   ④   ④   4

6   6   ⑤   ⑤   5   5   ④   –   6   6   ⑤   ⑤   5   5   ④

4   4   6   6   ⑥   ⑥   6   –   ⑤   ⑤   5   5   ④   ④   4

ARE YOU SLEEPING

4   ④   5   4   4   ④   5   4   –   5   ⑤   6   –   5   ⑤   6

6   ⑥   6   ⑤   5   4   6   ⑥   6   ⑤   5   4

4   3   4   –   4   3   4

ROW ROW ROW YOUR BOAT

4   4   4   ④   5   5   ④   5   ⑤   6   –   7   7   7   6   6   6   5   5   5   4   4   4

6   ⑤   5   ④   4

ON TOP OF OLD SMOKEY

4	4	5	6	7	(6)	(6)
(5)	6	(6)	6			
6	4	5	6	6	(4)	(4)	5	(5)	5	(4)	4

4   4   5   6   7   (6)   (6)
(5)   6   (6)   6
6   4   5   6   6   (4)   (4)   5   (5)   5   (4)   4

JINGLE BELLS

5   5   5   –   5   5   5   –   5   6   4   (4)   5
(5)   (5)   (5)   (5)   (5)   5   5   5   5   5   (4)   (4)   5   (4)   6
5   5   5   –   5   5   5   –   5   6   4   (4)   5
(5)   (5)   (5)   (5)   (5)   5   5   5   5   6   6   (5)   (4)   4

O SUSANNA

4   (4)   5   6   6   (6)   6   5   4   (4)   5   5   (4)   4   (4)
4   (4)   5   6   6   (6)   6   5   4   (4)   5   5   (4)   (4)   4
4   (4)   5   6   6   (6)   6   5   4   (4)   5   5   (4)   4   (4)
4   (4)   5   6   6   (6)   6   5   4   (4)   5   5   (4)   (4)   4
(5)   (5)   (6)   (6)   (6)   6   6   5   4   (4)
4   (4)   5   6   6   (6)   6   5   4   (4)   5   5   (4)   (4)   4

KUM BAH YAH

4   5   6   6   6   (6)   (6)   6
4   5   6   6   6   (5)   5   (4)
4   5   6   6   6   (6)   (6)   6
(5)   5   4   (4)   (4)   4

WHEN THE SAINTS GO MARCHING IN

4   5   (5)   6   4   5   (5)   6
4   5   (5)   6   5   4   5   (4)
5   5   (4)   4   4   5   6   6   6   (5)
5   (5)   6   5   4   (4)   4

MICHAEL ROW THE BOAT ASHORE

4   5   6   5   6   (6)   6   5   6   (6)   6
5   6   6   5   (5)   5   (4)   4   (4)   5   (4)   4

Other Classroom Instruments

The harmonica is only one of many classroom instruments that provide pleasure as well as pathways to learning. Others include Autoharp, resonator bells, song bells, hand bells, recorders, ukuleles, portable keyboards, and more. Among the more recent additions are "boomwhackers"(varied lengths of colored plastic tubing that produce different pitches when struck against a firm surface) and chime bars ("a hardier" version of hand bells). All of these instruments are available from suppliers who specialize in instruments designed for classroom use. (See Resources.)

Presenting a Music Listening Experience

It has been said that nowhere else are good listening skills more rewarded than in the art of music. Sadly, much of the population appear to be "musically deprived" because of poor listening habits. As one person put it, "Listening, to some people, means that their ears happened to be in the path of the sound."

The following ear training activities are offered here as introductory devices for improving musical acuity as well as for sharpening listening skills in general. It is suggested that they be engaged in before any larger listening experiences are attempted. In the process, it is hoped that establishing the habit of attentive listening at the outset will serve to enrich future aesthetic musical experiences.

Introductory Ear Training Activities

1. Try some echo clapping: clap short rhythm patterns and have children imitate.

2. Play a musical selection of your choice. Have children clap until the music stops. (Stop in unexpected places to increase attention.)

3. Coordinate visual representations that represent *high* and *low* (pictures of animals, buildings, etc.) with high and low tones in music. As each high or low musical tone is sounded, child answers by indicating an appropriate visual.

4. a. Repeat as in no. 2 above using pictures of *fast* or *slow* moving things (turtle, rabbit) and coordinate with music that is either fast or slow.
   b. Clap or beat a slow rhythm with children, and then gradually increase tempo having them follow the beat from slow to fast. Reverse, starting with a fast beat to slow.
   c. Have children identify fast and slow in various pieces played. In musical selections that contain both fast and slow sections have the children indicate (through some prearranged response) where the changes occur.

5. Repeat as in nos. 2 and 3 above using visuals that portray *up* and *down* (e.g., figure on a ladder, Jack and Jill, etc). Coordinate with short musical passages that go up or down. These need be only a few notes going in either

direction and may be sounded vocally or on song/resonator bells, keyboard, or other available instrument. (No talent required!)

6. Play two musical tones, and have the children identify whether they are the *same* or *different*. Same and different visual images may be used to motivate answers in this exercise in the same manner as no. 4 above.

7. Repeat no. 5 using short rhythm patterns sounded for identifying same or different:

♩ ♪♪♩ ♩   and   ♩ ♪♪♩ ♩

8. Repeat as in nos. 6 and 7 above using short melody excerpts (no particular tune) played on any melody instrument for identifying same or different.

9. Have children identify music that is *soft* or *loud* (e.g., march, lullaby).

10. a. When children have built a repertoire of songs, have them identify the name of a particular song from a melody excerpt sounded.

   b. Repeat as above, substituting the sound of the "melody rhythm" (every syllable of the words) for the tune. This may be done by clapping or with sticks, drum, or other suitable rhythm instrument.

Instruments of the Orchestra

Preparation for listening to musical masterpieces is well served by gaining familiarity with the instrruments that produce the various intriguing sounds heard in large symphonic works. Even very young children can learn to recognize some of them by sight as well as sound when presented a few at a time.

   A symphony orchestra is composed of instruments producing many different timbres. Traditionally, these instruments are grouped into "choirs" or sections according to the method of playing. The largest of these groups is the strings.

STRINGS

The string section consists of violins, violas, violoncellos (cellos), and bass viols, all played by drawing a bow over the strings. The *violin*—smallest of the string group—produces the highest sound. As with all instruments, size is related to pitch—the smaller the instrument, the higher the sound it produces; the larger the instrument, the lower the sound.

Violin   Viola

The *viola* is slightly larger in size than the violin, so it is lower in pitch. Both of these instruments are held under the chin resting on the shoulder for playing. Because the cello is too large to hold in this manner, it rests against the player's knee, supported by a device that allows it to stand on the floor. Because it is larger than the viola, its sound is lower.

Cello   Bass Viol

The *bass viol*, largest and lowest sounding of all the strings, stands on the floor with the player either standing or sitting on a high stool to play. The bass viol is also known by other names, including double bass, bass fiddle, string bass, and just plain bass. On all string instruments, different pitches are produced by placing the fingers in various positions on each string. For a different musical effect, strings may be plucked as well as bowed. This plucking is known as *pizzicato*.

The *harp* is also considered to be a member of the string section of the orchestra; however, it is played only by plucking and not with a bow.

Harp

WOODWINDS

Woodwind instruments are those on which the sound is made by blowing—not bowing.

The *piccolo* is the smallest and highest sounding of the woodwinds. The *flute* is slightly larger and lower sounding. Both of these instruments are held to one side in a horizontal playing position while blowing across an opening to sound a tone. The remaining woodwinds are divided into two classes—*single reed* and *double reed*.

Flute   Piccolo

The *single reed* instruments are those that have a single piece of cane as part of the mouthpiece. They include the *clarinet* and the larger *bass clarinet*, which bears some resemblance to a saxophone. Although classified as a single reed instrument, the saxophone is more traditionally associated with bands than with symphony orchestras. It should be noted, however, that some symphonic works for orchestra have been written to include saxophones in the scores.

Martha Ruskai/North Carolina School of the Arts

Clarinet   Bass Clarinet

The *double reed* instruments—*oboe, English horn, bassoon,* and *contrabassoon*—are those on which the mouthpiece consists of two pieces of cane attached together. This produces a distinctively different tone quality that we sometimes associate with "snake charmer" music. The oboe is the highest sounding of the double reeds, whereas the contrabassoon is the lowest. Although the sound range of these instruments varies widely, depending on their size, their distinctive quality is still discernible. Unlike the flute and piccolo, single and double reed instruments require a vertical holding position with the lips closing over a portion of the mouthpiece to blow. On all woodwind instruments, different tones are produced by pressing various keys.

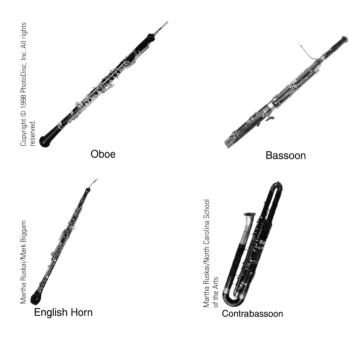

Oboe

Bassoon

English Horn

Contrabassoon

BRASS

Brass instruments in a symphony orchestra include *trumpet, French horn, trombone*, and *tuba*. Unlike woodwinds, brasses have no reeds, only a cup-like mouthpiece against which the lips are pressed and into which air is blown to produce a tone. With the exception of the trombone, pitches are varied by pressing down on different valves. Because the number of valves is limited, the range of pitches may be extended by tightening or loosening the lips to produce higher or lower tones, respectively. On the trombone, changing pitches is dependent upon the movement of a slide in place of valves. Extending the slide fully produces the longest air column and the resulting lowest tone for that instrument.

Trumpet

Tuba

Trombone

The *French horn* is the direct descendant of the old hunting horn and possesses a mellow tone, much less brilliant than that of the trumpet. In addition to pressing valves, a French horn player may also produce different tones by inserting the right hand into the bell of the instrument.

French Horn

The highest sounding instrument of the brass group is the trumpet—one of the oldest instruments in the world. The lowest sounding is the tuba.

PERCUSSION

Percussion instruments are those that are usually played by striking. Many of these instruments such as the *wood block, snare drum,* and *cymbals* have no definite pitch. The *kettledrums* or *tympani* (tim-pah-nee) may be tuned to desired pitches to accommodate the key of the given musical selection being performed.

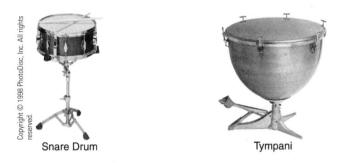

Snare Drum   Tympani

Melodic percussion are pitched percussion instruments on which melodies may be played. They include *xylophone, chimes, bells,* and *celesta.*

Xylophone

Folk/Ethnic Instruments

The term "instruments" embraces more than simply instruments of the orchestra. It also refers to the folk/ethnic instruments of cultures different from our own as well as those associated with particular regions of the United States. In addition to their intrinsic value, ethnic instruments can be fine teaching tools in the classroom because they tell us much about the people who played them, the places from where they originated and some of the uncommon ways in which they were used.

Those who specialize in the study of world music (ethnomusicologists) tend to group instruments in ways different from our familiar "strings" "woodwinds" etc., allowing the more "worldly" inclusion of many ethnic instruments. For example, the Chinese *sheng* is included under *aerophones* along with the woodwinds, brasses, and others. Classed as chordophones are all those we think of as strings with the addition of lutes, mandolins, balalaikas, and banjos. *Idiophones* seem like our percussion instruments until we note the washboard and Turkish crescent numbered among them. Drums of all types fall under the heading of *membranophones* and as the name implies, all that belong to this group are covered with membrane.

Children may be surprised to learn that many of our present day orchestral instruments are derived from ancient instruments of other lands. In this connection it should be noted that the Metropolitan Museum has a Department of Musical Instruments representing those from six continents as well as the Pacific Islands and dating from 300 BC to the present. What stories they could tell us!

Larger Listening Experience

An "aesthetic musical experience" requires that all children be "tuned in" (active listening) and that they have something to listen for (listening focus). A listening focus is determined by the stated objectives for the activity. For example, it may be in the form of a musical element (melody, form, etc.) or other music learning such as instruments of the orchestra. Whatever focus is chosen, all procedures should relate in some manner to the achievement of the objectives. In this connection, motivating children to listen to the piece selected heads the list.

MOTIVATING DEVICES

The following are merely suggestions and are included here because they touch upon other areas of the curriculum. Choice will obviously depend upon the grade level and the content of the music selected for the listening experience.

1. Making reference to:
   a. Topics currently under study in other subjects
   b. Events in children's immediate lives
   c. Upcoming holiday, seasonal event, or special day

2. Reading:
   a. Story, poem, legend, folk tale, or other literary piece upon which the music may be based or that contains similar subject matter

3. Showing:
   a. An ethnic instrument, costume, or other article of folk origin
   b. A painting or other artwork related in some manner to the listening selection
   c. Puppets, toys, or other objects portrayed in or otherwise related to the music

Listening experiences can provide many opportunities for creative expression in the form of dramatization, visual representations, movement/dance, as well as other related activities such as the selection of certain rhythm instruments to play in designated parts of the music.

Since many large musical works are related to historical events, nature, animals/creatures, folklore, and other areas, teachers are encouraged to enlarge their own listening repertoires so that possible linkages to other subjects may become more evident and interest deepened.

In summary, *Sorcerer's Apprentice* represents an abbreviated example of suggested procedure, sequence, and content of a larger listening experience. It is expected that its skeletal form will be fleshed out by creative teachers who will surely make more connections.

Sorcerer's Apprentice

Composer: Paul Dukas (1865–1935) French

Motivation: Read/tell story (Presence of a sorcerer may stir thoughts of Halloween)

This is an ancient tale, told in many lands, of a magician and his young assistant. Having observed his master performing magic feats, the assistant is eager to try some magic of his own, despite having been warned not to do so. One day when the magician is away, the boy recalls an incantation he has heard the magician use and tries it on a broom, commanding the broom to carry water from the well into the magician's house. To his happy surprise, the broom obeys; however, when enough water has been carried, the boy is unable to make it stop since he doesn't know the magic words to make it

Music Listening Selections

The following titles represent a broad range of music genres, composers and periods frequently found in music listening libraries prepared especially for schools. (See Resources.) These publications also include teaching guides containing helpful background information as well as suggestions for presenting the music in the classroom.

FAIRY TALES IN MUSIC

Cinderella—Prokofiev
Cinderella—Coates
Hansel and Gretel—Humperdinck
Mother Goose Suite—Ravel (Beauty and the Beast, etc.)
Three Bears—Coates
Once Upon a Time Suite—Donaldson (Three Billy Goats Gruff, Chicken Little, etc.)
Nutcracker Suite—Tschaikovsky
Sleeping Beauty—Tschaikovsky

MUSIC BASED ON LITERATURE/FOLK TALES/LEGENDS/MYTHS, ETC.

Love for Three Oranges—Prokofiev
Overture to William Tell—Rossini
Peer Gynt—Grieg
Red Pony Suite—Copland
Scheherazade—Rimsky-Korsakov
Midsummer Night's Dream—Mendelssohn
Billy the Kid—Copland
Amahl and the Night Visitors—Gian Carlo-Menotti
Help! Help! The Globolinks—Gian Carlo-Menotti
Sorcerer's Apprentice—Dukas
The Firebird—Stravinsky
Peter and the Wolf—Prokofiev
The Snow Maiden—Rimsky-Korsakov
Through the Looking Glass—Taylor
Till Eulenspiegel's Merry Pranks—R. Strauss
Firebird—Stravinsky
Danse Macabre—Saint Saëns
Mother Goose Suite—Ravel
Rodeo—Copland
Overture to Hansel and Gretel—Humperdinck

MUSIC THAT DESCRIBES A SCENE, HISTORICAL EVENT, PERSON, CREATURE, OR OBJECT

La Mer—Debussy
A Lincoln Portrait—Copland
The Moldau—Smetana

Pictures at an Exhibition—Moussorgsky
Wild Horseman—Schumann
Grand Canyon Suite—Grofé
Death Valley Suite—Grofé
Mississippi Suite—Grofé
Carnival of the Animals—Saint-Saëns
Night on Bald Mountain—Moussorgsky
1812 Overture—Tschaikovsky
The White Peacock—Griffas
Brer Rabbit—MacDowell
Viennese Musical Clock (from Hary Janos Suite)—Kodály
Little Windmills—Couperin
Music Box—Liadov
Flight of the Bumblebee—Rimsky-Korsakov
Hary Janos Suite—Kodály
Academic Festival Overture—Brahms
The Moldau—Smetan
An American in Paris—Gershwin
Clair de Lune—Debussy
Children's Corner Suite—Debussy

OTHER RECOMMENDED LISTENING

Young People's Guide to the Orchestra—Britten
Little Fugue in G Minor—Bach
Hallelujah Choirus from the Messiah—Handel
Eine Kleine Nachtmusik—Mozart
American Salute—Gould (Variations on When Johnny Comes
Marching Home)
Minute Waltz—Chopin

Selected movements from the following symphonies:
Symphony No. 5—Beethoven
Symphony No. 40—Mozart
Symphony No. 94—(Surprise) Haydn
Children's Symphony—McDonald

Selections from the following operas:
Carmen—Bizet
Marriage of Figaro—Mozart
Porgy and Bess—Gershwin

In addition to the foregoing there is also a wealth of recorded folk/ethnic music available to help children further understand ways of life among different cultures including their own. In this connection they may take pride in knowing that *jazz* is this country's unique contribution to the entire world of music.

stop. In a panic, he splits the broom in two, but only succeeds in creating another broom that immediately joins the water brigade. The result is a flood of rushing water, in the midst of which the magician returns, stops the brooms, and scolds the boy for disobeying orders.

Have children listen for:

- Magic incantation of the magician played by the brasses
- The marching brooms portrayed by the bassoon
- Musical devices used to portray the excitement of the flood
- Musical cues heard that signify the return of the magician and the subsiding of the waters

Post-listening discussion:

- Evaluate the composer's choice of instruments and other musical elements to portray the story
- Elicit suggestions for different musical ways of presenting the story

Related activities:

- Listen to other selections based on legends/folk tales, for example, *Danse Macabre* (Saint-Saëns) and *Night on Bald Mountain* (Moussorgsky)
- Identify portions of the music that could be accompanied by rhythm instruments and select the most appropriate instruments for the activity
- Explore some magic tricks
- Research the history of magic

Opportunities for creative expression:

- Dramatize the story
- Draw or paint any desired scene in the story
- Write a poem about the story or the composer's musical interpretation of it
- Choreograph a "dance of the brooms"

In summary, engaging in activities associated with listening experiences requires active listening, which, in turn, deepens involvement in the music.

A gentle reminder: Asking children to give their best listening attention to the music means that the teacher must do the same.

Music Reading

The proper time for introducing music reading to children is a frequently debated topic among music educators. One of the most familiar names mentioned is bound to be that of Hungarian composer/music educator Zoltan Kodaly.

The Kodaly method, now widely used in the United States and elsewhere, begins with learning songs based on the musical progressions commonly heard in children's play chants. Once the songs are learned, syllable names of the notes are incorporated along with Curwen hand signals (developed earlier by John Curwen) and rhythm syllables (ta, ti, etc.) designed to facilitate the reading of rhythmic notation.

Most of the songs used by Kodaly were classed as "pentatonic" meaning they were based on the pentatonic or 5-tone scale containing only the tones DO RE MI SOL LA. A pentatonic scale may be easily executed on any keyboard instrument by locating the recurring group of 5 black keys, then playing the first group of 3 followed by the group of 2. It is possible to play many well-known tunes using just those 5 keys ("Old MacDonald," "Auld Lang Syne," "Amazing Grace," and others). By any system learning to read music necessitates acquiring numerous musical skills, and is generally considered best left to those who specialize; thus, the information that follows is limited to what may serve as possible tools for facilitating some of the suggested activities mentioned in this chapter and others.

Simple songs such as those shown below built on tones of the ascending and descending major **scale** offer an appropriate introduction to learning the names of the scale tones:

Ascending: DO	RE	MI	FA	SOL	LA	TI	DO
Descending: DO	TI	LA	SOL	FA	MI	RE	DO

Ebeneezer Sneezer
Words and Music by Lynn Freeman Olson

Used by permission of Belwin-Mills Publishers.

Five Little Monkeys

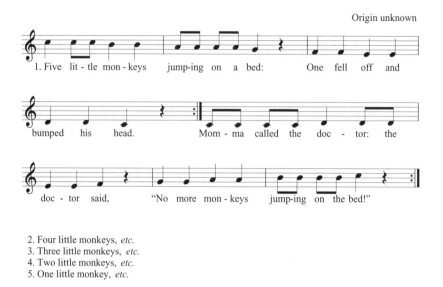

2. Four little monkeys, *etc.*
3. Three little monkeys, *etc.*
4. Two little monkeys, *etc.*
5. One little monkey, *etc.*

(When all the verses above have been sung using the descending tune, sing ascending tune "Momma called," etc.)

Responding with appropriate directional body movements to the sound of ascending or descending pitch levels can enhance not only the learning of the scale syllables but also the concepts of up or down and high or low. Scales may also be represented through visual images that could take various forms, depending on the children's impulses.

Using scale syllables to read melodies from the staff *independently* may begin as early as first grade. Following a planned sequence in each grade level, by sixth grade it is possible for these early learners to accomplish reading three-part harmony at sight.

Within the context of music, the term *rhythm* is frequently associated with "beat"; however, in a larger sense, rhythm constitutes the "regular recurrence of something." In the classroom, viewing rhythm in that context can lead to discussion concerning rhythm in life, in the universe, and in other arts. Heartbeats and walking are rhythmical, as are the tides, the seasons, and night/day. In dance, rhythm keeps us in step; in art, rhythm means patterns made by repeated elements (lines and shapes) that form "rhythms for the eyes." Countries and cities have distinguishable rhythms as do the individuals and animals that inhabit them. A person's particular rhythm can affect social relationships as well as his/her behavior on the freeways, which, incidentally, also have their own rhythms. In light of the foregoing, it would appear then that exploring rhythm with children can take us to many places.

Applied specifically to music, the "regularly recurring something" is *accent,* and we like it better when it occurs according to expectation, such as on the first of every 2, 3, 4, or even 6 beats.

Experiencing the "feel" of rhythm usually precedes the understanding and execution of it. "Let's Get the Rhythm" shown on pp. 145–146 is a good beginning.

For practice in feeling accent (and meter), execute one movement on each of the accented beats of the music heard and a different one on the unaccented ones, for example, in 3s—clap pat pat. This can also be experienced through performing conducting patterns—the same ones that conductors use when leading orchestras, bands, and choruses. The pattern used is determined by the upper figure of the meter signature (2,3,4, etc.), as shown below:

CONDUCTING

Some individuals mistakenly think that conductors are simply "keeping time" to the music played, when in fact they are *setting* the desired tempo, leading the musicians in all the nuances intended by the composer while at the same time artfully weaving in their own personal interpretations of the music. As conductor James Conlon was heard to say, "The function of a conductor is to unify a very diversified group of players."

One way to help maintain the steady beat of any given meter is to practice standard **conducting patterns**. The upper figure of the meter signature determines the appropriate hand directions. Commonly accepted as basic conducting patterns are those shown below:

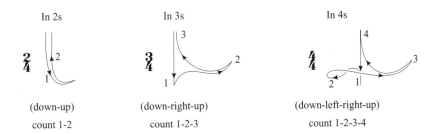

In 2s	In 3s	In 4s
(down-up)	(down-right-up)	(down-left-right-up)
count 1-2	count 1-2-3	count 1-2-3-4

Conductors most often use their right hand to execute the patterns shown above, leaving the left hand free to control dynamics (softs, louds, climaxes) and phrasing as well as to cue in the entrances of various instruments. (Not everyone plays all the time.)

The meaning of such musical terms as *crescendo* and *diminuendo* associated with dynamics may be reinforced through having children explore the art of conducting—even without an orchestra. Select a student conductor. Have class choose a word, saying it as softly as possible. Rise in volume, then lower as directed by the conductor. Repeat several times. If desired, children may rise slowly from their seats as the volume rises. In place of speaking, try singing the word on a musical tone. Call attention to the need for a deep breath at the outset in order to sustain the tone.

READING RHYTHMS

Reading rhythmic notation requires being able to maintain a steady beat (not fast on the easy parts/slow on the harder ones as in early piano lessons), and to interpret the notes/rests representing the sounds/silences that ride over the basic pulse. Using different sound syllables for different notes can help:

Some children's names can also be matched to rhythms, for example, a quarter note for the one syllable; two eighth notes for two syllables:

In sounding short rhythm patters for identification, answers initially can be in the form of names specified or by the tah and ti sounds; eventually, naming the kind of notes (quarter/eighth) sounded.

A little math comes into play as well, since the time value of the quarter note (♩) is equal to that of two eight notes (♪ ♪) and a half note (♩) is equal to two quarter notes. (See p. 108.) For more on musical signs and symbols, see below.

Eighth notes may be written with flags (♪ ♪) or barred when they appear in 2s or more (♫), (♫♫). Appearance does not affect the sound.

Summary of Musical Symbols

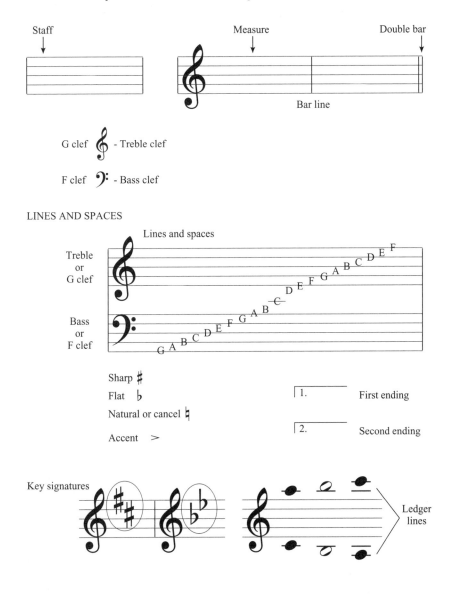

Staff

Measure

Double bar

Bar line

G clef 𝄞 - Treble clef

F clef 𝄢 - Bass clef

LINES AND SPACES

Lines and spaces

Treble
or
G clef

Bass
or
F clef

Sharp ♯

Flat ♭

Natural or cancel ♮

Accent >

1. First ending

2. Second ending

Key signatures

Ledger
lines

Meter signature

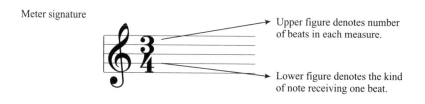

Upper figure denotes number of beats in each measure.

Lower figure denotes the kind of note receiving one beat.

Tempo—rate of speed

Crescendo		Gradually growing louder.
Diminuendo		Gradually growing softer.
Accelerando		Gradually getting faster (accel.)
Ritardando		Gradually getting slower (ritard.)
Legato		Smooth, flowing
Staccato		Short, detached

SOUND

♩ = Quarter note

♩ = Half note

𝗈 = Whole note

♪ = Eighth note

♬ = Sixteenth note

♩. = Dotted half note

♩. = Dotted quarter note

♪. = Dotted eighth note

SILENCE

𝄽 = Quarter rest

▬ = Half rest

▬ = Whole rest

𝄾 = Eighth rest

𝄿 = Sixteenth rest

In summary, if young people are to become aware of the power of music and its capacity to effect a significant emotional response, they must be given opportunities to explore all of its pathways through singing, playing, listening, moving, and creating.

RELATING MUSIC AND ART

Music and art have been close companions for centuries—even before Sir Isaac Newton began equating light rays with the sounds of musical tones (red with C, yellow with E, etc.).

Since then, many notable examples of relating these arts have emerged—in particular, composer Modest Mussorgsky's "Pictures at an Exhibition"—a musical intepretation of ten art works created by his friend and artist Victor Hartmann who had died earlier. A similar music–art partnership is represented in composer Gunther Schuller's "Seven Studies on the Themes of Paul Klee."

A more recent example played out on Broadway in the Stephen Sondheim musical "Sunday in the Park with George" based on one painting titled "A Sunday on La Grande Jatte" by artist Georges Seurat.

Mary Kuzniar of the Art Institute of Chicago writes, "Examining music and art together can highlight distinctive elements of each form. Yet, at the same time it can also demonstrate how their characteristics are interrelated." She goes on to suggest that when studying art, children be invited to "hear" the sounds depicted by various objects in a given painting, and to reproduce them in various ways (voice, rhythm instruments, other).[6]

In the classroom, listening to the music of these composers while viewing the paintings may not only widen children's arts horizons but also may provide opportunities for them to express their opinions on the composer's interpretation of a given art piece, the selection of instruments and other musical considerations. Depending on the content of the art work, this activity may also spark discussion on topics related to other subject areas. Finally, artist Joan Miro observes, ". . . when I paint I never really know what I will paint. I look at the many colors before me. I look at my blank canvas. Then, I try to apply colors like words that shape poems, like notes that shape music."

FOR DISCUSSION

1. What color do you feel best describes the sound of a flute? a tuba? a cello?
2. What instrument do you hear when you see the color yellow?
3. How might families of orchestral instruments be related to families of color in art?
4. It has been said that composers have "palettes" just as artists do. What kinds of choices would be on the composer's palette? Compare it to the artist's.
5. Emphasis in art means that a viewer's attention will be centered more on certain parts of the visual image than others. How does a composer achieve focal points or emphasis in a musical composition?
6. Visual rhythm in art depends on the repetition of certain elements. Upon what does rhythm in music depend?

7. Open spaces in art are as important as solids and planned as carefully. To what might these be compared in music?

Activities

1. Discover musical instruments shown in various art works representing different periods and cultures, e.g., harps in old Egyptian wall paintings and others.

2. Express a musical listening experience through selected art media using any style desired.

3. Create a visual representation of any one or more of the small musical forms such as ABA, theme and variations, rondo, fugue, and others.

4. Execute a mural inspired by a musical suite, for example, Peer Gynt (Grieg), Nutcracker (Tschaikovsky), or Firebird (Stravinsky) through sequential drawings on large roll-type or other similar paper. Contrasts in mood may be reflected in the choice of colors, types of strokes, and other ways.

5. Listen to music representing various periods and styles while viewing corresponding artworks.

6. Create designs inspired by music in contrasting meters, for example, duple, triple, and so on.

7. Create border designs inspired by music of various types, for example, march, waltz, and so on.

8. Represent any instrument of the orchestra in abstract, using an art medium of choice.

9. Listen to an unfamiliar musical selection. Create a story that seems to reflect the music, and then illustrate the story.

10. Design sets for a musical production by the class.

11. Listen to musical compositions inspired by artists' works, for example, *Seven Studies on Themes of Paul Klee* (Gunther Schuller), *Isle of the Dead* (Rachmaninoff), *Pictures at an Exhibition* (Mussorgsky), and others.

12. Illustrate scenes portrayed in music, for example, "Festival of Baghdad" from *Scheherazade* (Rimsky-Korsakov).

13. Refer to the conducting patterns on p. 105. Notice how each forms a particular configuration. Using any one of the patterns as a base, create a design in color on the pattern.

14. Compose an imaginary musical selection using only color and shapes of any material desired and no musical symbols or sound. Indicate appropriate dynamics (soft, loud, etc.) through variety in form and hue. Have viewers "interpret" the composition as they see (and "hear") it.

15. "Orchestrate" a painting or drawing by reproducing some of its elements or visual effects in sound—for example, different kinds of brush strokes, brilliant colors, or strong contrast.

— NATIONAL STANDARDS — GRADES K–8

Content Standards

1. Singing, alone and with others, a varied repertoire of music.
2. Performing on instruments, alone and with others, a varied repertoire of music.
3. Improvising melodies, variation, and accompaniment.
4. Composing and arranging music within specified guidelines.
5. Reading and notating music.
6. Listening to, analyzing, and describing music.
7. Evaluating music and music performances.
8. Understanding relationships between music, the other arts, and disciplines outside the arts.
9. Understanding music in relation to history and culture.

Source: Excerpted from *National Standards for Arts Education*, published by Music Educators National Conference (MENC). Copyright 1994 by MENC. Used by permission. The complete National Arts Standards and additional materials relating to the Standards are available from MENC—The National Association for Music Education, 1806 Robert Fulton Drive, Reston, VA 2091 (Telephone 800-336-3768).

Content standards, as shown above, are expected to be achieved through a variety of musical activities including singing in unison, in parts, and in other languages; playing classroom instruments; reading/interpreting musical signs and symbols; moving to music; listening to vocal and instrumental music by master composers for recognition of voices, musical elements, instruments of the orchestra, and more; creating original music; discovering the role of music in other cultures; and identifying musical connections with related arts and other classroom disciplines.

— GLOSSARY —

A capella: Singing without accompaniment.
Alto: Lowest child's or woman's voice. Also, a part within a certain musical range, whether played or sung.
Bar lines: Vertical lines drawn at measured distances on the staff to divide it into measures.

Bass: Lowest male voice. Also, a part within a certain musical range, whether played or sung.

Bass clef: Denotes lower register than treble clef; clef from which lower pitched voices and instruments sing and play. First line of staff bearing this symbol is G.

Binary: Two-part form consisting of two contrasting sections, designated AB.

Canon: A musical form in which a given melody is imitated by two or more voices beginning at different times.

Chord: Three or more tones sounded simultaneously.

Chorus: A group of people singing together; a composition written for combined voices. Also, the part of a song that is repeated after each verse.

Concerto: A symphonic composition written for solo or group of instruments and orchestra, usually consisting of three contrasting movements.

Conducting patterns: Arm movements used by conductors as determined by the meter signature of a musical composition.

Conductor: Person who directs a chorus, orchestra, band, or other musical group.

Consonance: A combination of tones that, when sounded simultaneously, produces a feeling of rest with no need for further resolution.

Crescendo: Gradually growing louder in sound.

Diminuendo: Gradually growing softer in sound.

Dissonance: A combination of tones that, when sounded simultaneously, produces a feeling of tension or unrest and a need for further resolution.

Double bar: Two vertical lines signifying the end of a section or a whole piece of music.

Duet: A musical performance by two voices or instruments.

Duple meter: Meter in which there are two beats or some multiple of two in each measure of the given musical piece.

Dynamics: Varying intensities of sound and climaxes in a musical composition.

Elements of music: Melody, harmony, rhythm, and form.

Flat: Musical symbol representing a tone one-half step below the note before which it is placed.

Folk song: Song usually of unknown origin, arising as an outgrowth of a culture and handed down through generations by oral tradition.

Form: The basic structure or design of a musical composition resulting from the arrangement of repetition, contrast, variation, or other manipulation of the material.

Found instruments: Any sound-producing object or combination of objects that may be struck, plucked, blown, or performed on in any other way acceptable to the player.

Fugue: Literally, "flight." A form involving two or more voices in which a musical subject (theme) is introduced and developed through a series of imitations.

Harmony: Sound resulting from the simultaneous sounding of two or more consonant tones.

Interval: The musical (pitch) distance between two tones.

Jazz: Twentieth-century musical style characterized by duple meter, syncopation, and improvisation. Considered to be America's unique contribution to the world of music.

Key: Refers to the specific tonality of a musical selection as determined by the keynote and the corresponding scale system.

Key signature: The group of sharps or flats found at the beginning of a piece of music (next to the clef) indicating the key (or scale) of the music. See "Summary of Musical Symbols," pp. 107–108.

Legato: Smooth, flowing. Opposite of *staccato*.

Measure: A space on a staff enclosed by two vertical bar lines.

Melody: A group of single tones arranged in a meaningful sequence.

Meter: A specified arrangement of beats within a measure.

Meter signature: A set of two numbers at the beginning of a piece of music (next to the key signature). The upper figure determines the number of beats in each measure; the lower figure determines the unit of beat (the kind of note that receives one beat.)

Examples include: 3   2   6
                     4   2   8

Mode: A specified arrangement of scale tones. Examples include minor, pentatonic, and others.

Music reading: Interpreting melodic and rhythmic symbols accurately (by voice or instrument) from a printed page of music.

Ostinato: A repeated melodic or rhythmic fragment occurring throughout a piece of music.

Out-of-tune singers: Those individuals who have difficulty matching given musical pitches, resulting in their singing "off key" or "out of tune."

Partner songs: Two or more songs that may be sung simultaneously because they contain parallel chord structure (i.e., designated chords coincide measure for measure) producing a pleasing, harmonious result.

Pentatonic scale: Universal five-tone scale consisting of scale tones DO RE MI SOL LA. May be sounded on the black keys of a keyboard instrument beginning on the first key of the group of three black (DO RE MI) and then ending with the group of two black (SOL LA.)

Phrase: A small section of a composition comprising a musical thought. Sometimes compared to a sentence in language.

Pitch: The highness or lowness of a tone, determined by the frequency of sound wave vibrations. Higher pitches result from a greater number of vibrations, lower pitches from fewer vibrations.

Rest: Musical symbol for silence. See "Summary of Musical Symbols," pp. 107–108.

Rhythm: Regular recurrence of accent; basic pulse underlying the long and short sounds and silences represented by note and rest symbols.

Rhythm instruments: In the context of this book, the term is used to refer to those instruments designed primarily for classroom use and include varieties of sticks, cymbals, tambourines, and others.

Rondo form: A musical form in which a recurring main theme (A) alternates with two or more secondary themes (B and C), designated ABACA.

Rote song: A song learned through the ear.

Round: A form of imitative singing in which voices enter at measured time intervals and sing the melody as many times as desired.

Scale: A graduated series of tones arranged in a specified order.

Sharp: A musical symbol representing a tone one-half step above the tone before which it is placed.

Soprano: Highest treble voice; also a part within a certain range, whether played by an instrument or sung.

Staccato: Sounded in a short, detached manner. Opposite of *legato*.

Staff: Five equally spaced horizontal lines and the four spaces between them upon which music is written.

Suite: An instrumental form that may consist of a group of dances, descriptive pieces or pieces from a ballet or opera, unified through a story or idea.

Symphony: A large musical work for orchestra consisting of several movements—usually four.

Tempo: Rate of speed at which a musical composition is performed.

Tenor: Highest male voice; also a part within a certain range, whether played by an instrument or sung.

Ternary: Three-part form consisting of a section of musical material designated A, followed by a contrasting section designated B, followed in turn by a repeat of the original A. Written ABA.

Texture: Determined by the presence or absence of harmony and arrangement of other musical components. Classified as *monophonic* (single line of melody with no accompaniment), *homophonic* (melody supported by vocal or instrumental chordal accompaniment), or *polyphonic* (several melodies sounded simultaneously, as in a round or fugue).

Theme: A short musical passage that states an idea, often providing the basis for variations or development in a musical composition. Also referred to as subject.

Theme and variations: Stated theme, subjected to various musical alterations such as change of key, meter, mode, instrumentation, and/or other form of modification.

Timbre: The quality of a musical tone that distinguishes various voices and instruments.

Time signature: See *meter signature*.

Tone: A musical sound; the quality of a musical sound.

Treble clef: Denotes higher register than bass clef; clef from which higher pitched voices and instruments sing and play. First line of staff bearing this symbol is E.

Triple meter: Meter in which there are three beats or some multiple of three in each measure of the given musical piece.

Variations: Different treatments of a given theme or melody through alterations in rhythm, mood, tempo, meter, and others.

See also "Summary of Musical Symbols," pp. 107–108.

— NOTES —

1. Used by permission of James Heup.
2. Roger Rideout, "Psychology and Music Education since 1950," *Music Educators Journal* (September 2002).
3. Don Campbell, *The Mozart Effect* (New York: Avon Books, 1997)
4. POEMS

   Richard Margolis, *Only the Moon and Me* (Philadelphia: Lippincott, 1969). Used by permission.

   Lucia and James L. Hymes, Jr., "Ears Hear," *Oodles of Noodles* (Glenview, IL: Pearson Education, 1964). Reprinted by permission of Pearson Education, Inc.

   Aileen Fischer, "I Like Weather," copyright 1963, 1991 by Aileen Fisher. Used with permission of Marian Reiner

   Annette Wynne, "The House Cat," *Days and Days* (Philadelphia: Lippincott, 1919).
5. Rudolph Chelminski, "Harmonicas Are Hooty, Wheezy, Twangy and Tooty," Smithsonian Magazine (November 1995).
6. Mary Kuzniar, "Finding Music In Art," *Music Educator's Journal* (December 1999).

— FOR FURTHER READING —

Anderson, William M., and Joy E. Lawrence. *Integrating Music into the Elementary Classroom*. Belmont, CA: Wadsworth Publishing, 1998.

Ardley, Neil. *The Science Book of Sound*. New York: Gulliver Books, Harcourt Brace Co., 1991.

Ayensu, Edward, and Philip Whitfield. *The Rhythms of Life*. Smithsonian Institute, Crown Publishing, 1981.

Bonny, H. L., and L. M. Savary. *Music and Your Mind*. Barrytown, NY: Station Hill Press, 1990.

Campbell, Don G. *Introduction to the Musical Brain*. Wheaton, IL: Theosophical Publishing House, 1983.

_____. *Music and Miracles*. Wheaton, IL: Theosophical Publishing House, 1992.

_____. *The Mozart Effect*. New York: Avon Books, 1997.

Cline, Dallas. *"Making Simple Folk Instruments for Children,"* Music Educator's Journal, February 1980.

DiBelli, Remo. "Drumming," Music Educator's Journal, December 2001.

Gelineau, R. Phyllis. *Understanding Music Fundamentals*, 2nd ed. Upper Saddle River, NJ: Prentice Hall, 1995.

_____. *Experiences in Music*, 3rd ed. Upper Saddle River, NJ: Prentice Hall, 1995.

Hart, Mickey. *Drumming at the Edge of Magic*. San Francisco: Harper, 1990.

"Junkyard Band," *National Geographic World* July 1981.

Kline, Tod. *Classic Tunes and Tales (Music Listening Lessons K–8)*. West Nyack, NY: Parker Publishing, 1997.

Levine, Shar, and Leslie Johnstone. *The Science of Sound and Music.* New York: Sterling Publishing Co., 2000.

Marsalis, Wynton. *Marsalis on Music.* New York: W. W. Norton, 1995.

_____. *Jazz for Youmg People Curriculum.* (Recordings, teacher and student guides, video). New York: Warner Books, 2001.

Musical Instruments. New York: Scholastic Inc., Voyages of Discovery, 1994.

Phillips, Kenneth H. *Teaching Kids to Sing.* New York: Shirmer Books, 1996.

Schonberg, H. C. *The Lives of the Great Composers*, 3rd ed. New York: W. W. Norton, 1997.

Stains, Bill. *All God's Critters Got a Place in the Choir*. New York: Puffin Books, 1978.

Tomatis, Alfred A., MD. *The Conscious Ear*. Paris: Editois Fixot, 1991.

— RESOURCES —

Videos

Marsalis, Wynton. *Why Toes Tap*. Teacher's Video Co., 1995.

Sing Dance and Sign (Video or recording and guide). See "Catalogues" (p. 117) for a wide selection.

The following are available from Films for Humanities and Sciences (See Catalogues.)

Listening to the Silence (African Cross Rhythms) 1996
Introduction to the Orchestra 1985
Dizzy Gillespie Bob and a Bent Trumpet 1998

Instrumental Suppliers

Rhythm Band Inc.
P. O. Box 126
Fort Worth, TX 76101
Tel: 1-800-784-9401

Suzuki
P. O. Box 261030
San Diego, CA 92196
Tel: 1-800-854-1594

West Music
P. O. Box 5521
Coralville, Iowa 52245
Tel: 1-800-397-9378

Catalogues

Teacher's Video
P. O. Box 4455-02MU04
Scottsdale, Arizona 85261
Tel: 1-800-262-8837
www.teacher'svideo.com

Educational Activities Inc.
P. O. Box 392
Freeport, NY
Tel: 1-800-645-3739
www.edact.com

Kimbo Dept. J
P. O. Box 47
Long Branch, NJ 07740-0477
Tel: 1-800-631-2187
www.kimboed.com

MMB Music Inc. (Creative Arts Therapy and General Music Catalogue)
3526 Washington Ave.
St. Louis, MO 63103-1019
Tel: 314-531-9635

Films for Humanities and Sciences
P. O. Box 2053
Princeton, NJ 08543-2053
Tel: 1-800-257-5126
www.films.com

Red Note Records
5049 Orange Port Road
Brewerton, NY 13029
(Publishers of Red Grammer song collections)

Music Libraries for Listening Selections

Adventures in Music
McGraw-Hill/Contemporary
4255 W. Touhy Ave.
Lincolnwood IL 60712
Tel: 1-800-323-4900
www.ntc-cb.com

Bowmar Orchestral Library
Warner Bros. Publications
15800 NW 48th Ave.
Miami, FL 33014-6422
http://warnerbrospub.com

Note: Try the Music Educator's website MENC.com for more resources, teaching aids, and information related to music education.

Basic Music Series

Making Music, Grades K–6, 2002.
The Music Connection, Grades 7–8, 2000.
Silver Burdett Ginn Scott Foresman, Glenview, IL.
800-552-2259

Share the Music, Grades K–8, 2000.
Macmillan/McGraw Hill, New York.
800-442-9865

Drama

When referring to this art form, many individuals tend to use the terms *drama* and *theatre* interchangeably; however, in his book *Development Through Drama* Brian Way makes a clear distinction—"theatre is largely concerned with communication between actors and an audience; drama is largely concerned with *experience* by the participants, irrespective of any function of communication to an audience." Way also adds "theatre is undoubtedly achievable with a very small minority, but drama, like the rest of education, is concerned with the majority."[1] In other words, the emphasis in drama is on personal development of the individual, not on the making of a production for an audience.

By any name, this art is an area of human expression that can provide greater insight into ourselves as human beings as well as deeper sensitivity to others. Concerned with the uniqueness of each individual, creative drama uses the facets of human beings that are already part of their "givens"—the five senses, imagination, physical body, speech, emotions, and intellect. In a sense, these could be considered the **elements of drama**—vehicles for providing experiences that foster creative, cognitive, social, emotional, and physical development. In addition, drama can increase the boundaries of imagination, sharpen intuition, improve concentration, and facilitate problem solving.

In summary, drama plays upon the entire self—mind, body, and emotions. Of all the arts, drama seems to call most upon these and the freeing of the spirit.

Experiencing Drama in the Classroom

. . . there is not a child born anywhere in the world in any physical or intellectual circumstances or conditions who cannot do drama . . . .

Brian Way

Extending into the human experience, drama teaches children about life—deeds and misdeeds, choices and consequences, how to do and undo, when to speak and when to be silent, as well as how to listen, imagine, and express creatively. Drama can develop better listening habits, provide emotional release, and refine social skills that facilitate getting along with others. Its processes can also help heighten sensitivity to the feelings of others, as well as respect for differing points of view, by allowing experimentation with different behaviors and resolution of conflict in a safe environment.

In addition to building self-confidence and expression skills, drama has proven to be a most fertile field for integration into other subject areas as well as a vitalizer of their content—enlivening literature, science, social studies, and more. In language arts, for example, drama can help children to speak and write more clearly, increase vocabulary, improve reading comprehension skills, and extend their repertoire of good literature. Moreover, drama's affinity with other arts makes it a key player in their domains.

For those whose classroom experience with creative drama borders on none, the following verse from *The Prophet* is worthy of reflection:

> If he is indeed wise he does not bid you enter the house of his wisdom, but rather leads you to the threshold of your own mind.[2]

Kahlil Gibran

Taking a cue from Gibran, author Frances Durland writes, "Your value as a teacher or leader in the world of education may be said to depend upon your ability to bring each child to the threshold of his/her own unique capacities. . . . There is no way to change the elements that go into the making of a unique personality, but there are ways to rearrange the pattern to better advantage."[3]

Although it is understood that, for the most part, drama activities will be teacher initiated, it is preferable that they not be teacher dominated—laced with too much "demonstration" of how and what; rather, each child should be allowed to find his/her own way in the process. It should be noted, however, that younger children will require more guidance at the outset.

Like most creative endeavors, drama in the classroom begins with attention to sensory impressions.

> . . . ideas and emotions growing out of sense impressions are the basis of man's living with himself and others, as well as the source of the creative imagination that underlies everything man has ever created of lasting worth in this world.[4]

Brian Way writes,

> Our sensitivity as people, our awareness of ourselves and the world about us and therefore our own personal enrichments in life are all partly dependent on developing our sensory instruments to the fullest extent of their powers. . . .[5]

Heightening awareness to sensory stimuli also aids in enabling individuals to recall the sensation when the stimulus is no longer there, allowing them to react believably through fitting facial expressions, words, and movement.

In brief, drama requires bringing the senses to a high level. To that end, many of the drama activities involve sensory experiences; thus, a prior discussion on ways to make the most of the senses might be helpful.

The drama-based activities on the following pages are drawn from a wide spectrum of classroom drama. It is hoped that teachers will experiment with those that seem appropriate in their present forms for a particular grade level, as well as venture into creating adaptations and modifications of others.

Warming Up

Depending on the grade level, some teachers may wish to precede selected drama activities with a **warm-up** that calls upon the body's mental as well as physical equipment. The following represent a small sample of many possible activities:

1. Shake out—beginning with fingers, then hands, arms, shoulders, head, one foot, other foot, hips, whole body.

2. Roll each shoulder in a circle—starting forward, then backward, then roll both shoulders at once in the same direction.

3. Lift the head as high as possible, then release.

4. Mentally feel one at a time—toes, legs, arms, torso, neck, head, ears, mouth, eyes, nose.

5. Raise arms over head one at a time. Stretch to reach the sky. Rise up on tiptoe to extend the reach.

6. Wave with various parts of the body—one finger, hand, arm, two arms, head, torso, whole body.

   a. As a variation, wave at someone in the same room, then someone outside in the backyard, then someone across the street.
   b. Pretend your car has stalled. Wave down the first vehicle that approaches.
   c. Pretend you're stranded on a desert island. Wave at a plane passing over for help.

Relaxing Exercises

When a break is needed to relax anytime during the day, try these:

1. Hold right arm straight out in front. Clench fist as tightly as possible. Retain position for five seconds, then release. Repeat with left arm, then with both arms. Hold one leg off the floor slightly forward. Tighten, hold, then release. Repeat with other leg.

   Tighten whole body, hold, then release.
   Tighten whole body, hold, then release.
   Give yourself a tight hug, hold, then release.
   Make a funny tight face, hold, then release.

2. Raise both arms over head.

   Drop one wrist, then the other.
   Drop one forearm, then the other.
   Drop remaining upper arm, then the other.

Drop head onto chest.
Drop full torso.

There are eight motions in this exercise that may be done to the eight tones of a descending scale if desired: DO TI LA SOL FA MI RE DO.

3. Imagine yourself a wooden board. Become rigid all over. Hold for five seconds and then change to being cooked spaghetti.

This tightening/loosening exercise may be done using other clues, depending on the grade level:

- Toy soldier to rag doll
- Ice to water

Invite suggestions from children about other objects fitting the categories that could be used as clues.

PANTOMIME

Pantomime (or simply, "mime") is generally thought of as acting without words; however, its history reveals it as something more. Originally a form of entertainment in Greek and Roman times, the "more" consisted of songs, dances, gymnastics, and juggling as well as short dramatic skits—frequently R-rated. Mythological, historical, or comical stories were danced by a major actor, supported by a chorus chanting the material and explaining the action. Although the Greeks record mime as early as sixth century B.C., the earliest Roman record is 211 B.C.

Since mime troupes were transients, they were forced to perform in any location they could create—courtyards, town squares, and other "found" spaces. This transience, combined with permitting women to play female roles, (an act previously prohibited) resulted in severe censure from the local communities. Furthermore, when the content moved from R-rated to X-rated, the Christian religious community rose up in protest, to which the troupes responded by ridiculing Christian beliefs and sacraments in their performances. As a result of these acts, it is believed that mime was the form largely responsible for strong Christian opposition to the theatre.

Today, mime is a respected art with many practitioners, including the internationally famous Marcel Marceau, whom critics consider the greatest of them all. Speaking of mime in connection with bodily/**kinesthetic** intelligence, Howard Gardner describes what is required: "It is up to the mime to create the *appearance* of an object, person or an action. . . . To depict an object . . . the mime has to delimit, by means of gestures, the shape of an object and to denote, by means of facial expressions and bodily actions, what that object is doing and its effects upon him." Of Marceau, Gardner writes,

> Marceau is able to create not only personalities (like a bully) and actions (like climbing) but also animals (butterflies), natural phenomena (waves cresting), and

even abstract concepts such as freedom or bondage, good or evil, ugliness or beauty. More amazingly . . . he often creates a number of these illusions simultaneously.[6]

Finding ways for children to view a performance by a recognized professional mime would be worth many bake sales. It is truly dramatic art at its finest.

In the classroom, pantomime can be a fruitful source of creative material and an "excellent means of learning detail of characterization because action, not words, must make the meaning clear to the audience." One is reminded of the old silent movies in which the character was forced to make broad gestures and exaggerate facial expressions to further the plot because there was no sound to play that part.

In its simplest form, pantomime is "most useful as a means of attaining spontaneity of bodily freedom." Because it may be done as a group exercise at the outset, it can also prove helpful in overcoming individual as well as group inhibitions.

In summary, mime requires close observation of the human race in all its conditions.

Activities

The following activities contain pantomime in some form that may be varied as desired. Numbers 1 through 4 may be done with the entire class—all doing the same task simultaneously:

1. Use different parts of the body to make familiar gestures (e.g., clap with your ankles, nod with your knees, say "no" with your left foot, laugh with your right foot, etc.)

2. Pantomime daily tasks such as eating various foods (apple, banana, pizza, etc.), brushing teeth, putting on socks and shoes, washing hands, and so on. Note: When guiding children's thinking in this area, it helps to remind them of all the preparatory movement that is involved before the task itself is actually performed (e.g., bananas must be peeled, apples do not; soap is needed for washing hands, etc.)

3. Pretend to:
   a. Be entangled in something
   b. Be trapped in a small enclosure that keeps growing smaller
   c. Walk upstairs
   d. Walk downstairs

4. Pretend to:

   a. Pitch a baseball
   b. Dribble a basketball
   c. Throw a football pass
   d. Jump rope
   e. Give the dog a bath
   f. Pull in a tug of war

Have the class originate other tasks to pantomime.

5. Create flashcards containing names of different actions (wash the dog), sensations (hot, cold), emotions (anger, joy), and objects (chair, tree). Hold them up for group to interpret.

6. As children become more comfortable with this form, they may be introduced to activities that embrace a broader variety of movement yet still remain comfortably within the large group setting.

Have one child leave the room. The class will decide on a setting (office, hospital, etc.) as well as a scene that will be portrayed. (Inanimate objects welcome too.) The child returns to guess the designated place and if desired may join the scene also.

7. Divide into small groups and assign each a destination (e.g., beach, camping, shopping mall). Allow planning time, and then have them portray the necessary preparations for their trips and the sensory experiences on arrival.

8. Set a scene by having a child (or the teacher) pantomime a recognizable activity (e.g., casting a fishing rod, painting a house, etc.). Ask children to fill in the scene (a few at a time) by choosing appropriate parts to play (worm, tree, ladder, etc.). Invite volunteers to initiate other scenes as desired and fill in as before.

9. Form a circle and pantomime passing balls of different sizes and substances as designated by teacher or child (e.g., ping-pong, medicine, hot, sticky, etc.). If desired, vary the tempo (slow, fast) of the passing.

10. Form a circle. The teacher begins the action by passing an imaginary (but identifiable) object to a child, who in turn transforms it into something different and passes it on. This passing/transformation continues around the circle. If the teacher feels that some children might not have been quite sure what each object was as passed, each child in circle may identify it when the circle is completed.

11. Divide into groups of two. Give each pair a card on which is written parts to play such as "painter and easel," "screw and screwdriver," "top and spinner," and "snowman and sun." Each pair decides its parts and pantomimes the action for others to guess.

12. Form a circle. Have the first child announce, "When I travel to Texas I'm going to take my _____." The object may be anything the child desires to take but is not mentioned—only pantomimed. The next child must repeat the sentence, pantomiming the preceding object and adding another. Repeat as many times as can be handled by the age group.

13. Divide the class into groups. Assign (by written card) each group an object to portray (e.g., Venetian blind, books and bookends, elastic band, etc.), and have others identify the object.

14. Write various motion activities on cards to put in a hat (e.g., pick apples, make a sandwich, etc.). Have each child take a card and perform the activity shown for others to guess.

15. Divide the class into groups of five or six. Instruct each group to become a form of transportation or "people mover" using no sound or movement. This will require arranging themselves in a configuration that resembles the form of transportation they choose to depict. Because other groups will be asked to identify the type of machine, there should be no discussion of examples by the teacher preceding the activity (FYI—aside from the usual plane, train, and bus, surprises do occur, e.g., elevator, escalator, and pack animal).

16. Using the same guidelines as those in no. 15 above:

a. Portray a household appliance of today. Movement is permitted but no sound. To vary, be a household appliance of 1776. Have others identify.
b. Portray a favorite food, using no movement and no sound—just the configuration for others to identify.
c. Be a statue representing an historic event, holiday, legend, fairy tale, or fable for others to identify.

Stories with several well-defined characters such as "Gingerbread Boy," "Chicken Little," "Three Little Pigs," and others lend themselves well to dramatization by younger children. They may be read by the teacher, with children pantomiming the appropriate action. Masks of the characters may be made and added, if desired.

Closely related to pantomime is the **tableau**. Like pantomime, a tableau is wordless, but unlike pantomime is also motionless—depicting only a "frozen" scene. Tableaux were more common in the past when they were used to portray religious subjects at holiday times. More recently they have been presented in art shows where the intent is to display an artwork using live human forms.

IMPROVISATION

Requiring no script, **improvisation** allows the bypassing of many barriers such as reading ability and memorization that often hamper a child's participation; thus, it may be explored and enjoyed by all. Its benefits in the classroom include improved communication skills as well as reenforcement of learnings in other disciplines, because the subject matter may be selected as desired.

Improvisation may begin with discussions of sensory experiences produced by various environments, emotions felt during certain events, as well as reactions in various happenings.

With children the teacher's part in the process is to remain sensitive to their initial suggestions then guide them to create their own material and interpretations. Moreover, in setting up situations that children will discuss and play out, it is necessary to provide them with sufficient planning time to ensure a well-defined beginning, middle, and end to the piece.

The following activities involve gesture, movement, characterization, improvisation, and other facets of drama and may be adapted or modified as desired for use in selected grade levels.

1. Mirror images are standard fare in drama because they require eye contact, which in turn builds rapport and sends the message. (One drama student reported doing this exercise three hours, twice a week for the whole semester.)

Before beginning, it is suggested that the class engage in various up/down, sideways, and other movements motivated by clues from the teacher such as:

- "Pull the rope that sounds the church bell."
- "Paint a wall from left to right only."
- "Paint the same wall up and down only."
- "Play a piece on the piano with both hands that uses the whole keyboard."
- "Reach for a star."
- "Paint the ceiling."

Initiate the mirror exercise with the teacher assuming the part of the person and the class the part of the mirror-reflecting (imitating) all the movements the teacher makes, then divide into pairs. Have children decide which parts they will play (mirror or person). Encourage concentration, slow movements and constant eye contact, and no conversation. Musical accompaniment (on the gentle side) is suggested. (Try *Canon in D* by Johann Pachabel.)

2. Also in pairs, have one child play the part of a marionette, and the other the operator who pulls the strings attached to each part of the marionette's body—fingers, hands, legs, and so on. The marionette responds appropriately.

3. Have children choose inanimate objects they wish to be and tell the class some facts about themselves.

4. Improvise a dialogue between an ant and a grasshopper in a high rise; do the same with a tortoise and a hare on the freeway.

5. Divide into groups. Have each group plan out a scene (with a beginning, middle, and end) using improvised dialogue and consisting only of the numbers 1 through 8 in place of words.

Do the same using gibberish in place of numbers or words.

6. Discuss the various interpretations provided by accenting a different word of the following sentence each time it is spoken: "Where are you going?" Create other sentences to try in the same manner.

7. Have a person assume a pose in a seated position, with one leg crossed over the other. Rest the arm on the knee and support the chin with the back of the hand. Place the other hand down beside the body in any position desired. Hold the head back and focus the eyes on ceiling.

Have everyone study the pose for ten seconds, and then ask for a volunteer to replace the person and re-create the pose. Repeat with other volunteers.

8. Divide into groups and assign each group a place and situation (e.g., stuck in an elevator, car break down on lonely road, etc.). Each group must discuss its predicament, choice of actors, and sequence of action and improvise dialogue to present the scene for others to guess its nature.

9. Create an original sound story containing well-defined characters. Determine the sounds appropriate for each character, and assign sounds to various groups. Read the narrative and have groups execute their sounds when the character is mentioned.

10. Improvise a conversation between two cavemen and a bear with an attitude problem.

11. Divide into pairs. Pass out cards showing names of two inanimate objects. Have pairs improvise dialogue between the objects (e.g., steak/grill, chainsaw/tree, Titanic/iceberg, back/front doors of house, parking space/car, etc.).

12. Divide into groups of five or six. Assign each group a different familiar fairy tale, fable, myth, or legend that they are to update into the present century. Decisions as to the role each child will play should be left to the group. Allow sufficient time for each group to discuss the content possibilities and then sketch out the sequence of events and improvise the dialogue. Using simple scenery and costumes can enhance the activity.

As a variation, have each group create its own original folk tale, fairy tale, or fable and proceed as before. Remind children that folk tales explain how things happen; fairy tales deal with fantasy, good/evil, and the supernatural; and fables revolve around morals and animals.

13. Divide into pairs—interviewer and interviewee. Set a time limit for the interview and then have the interviewer report to the class what he/she has learned about the other person.

14. Divide into groups. Have each group select a favorite painting and then bring it to life with sound, movement, and dialogue. Some simple costuming (and perhaps props) will enhance the presentation.

15. Call out a scene to represent (e.g., beach) and then count from one to ten as volunteers fill in the scene with the appropriate activity or pose within the time limit. Freeze the motion and then call out another scene (e.g., office). Repeat as before, ending with freeze.

16. Have the class become angry in ten counts, saying each number out loud and increasing the intensity with each succeeding number. Cool down by saying numbers in reverse, decreasing intensity as they lower.

17. Construct a "feeling" wheel, with different emotions written on the surface. Have children spin the wheel and display the emotion written on the stopping place.

18. Create a paper bag mask (this mask is not expected to be worn) representing a creature, monster, alien, or any other character of choice. When mask is completed, form several groups that consist of a variety of the characters shown and then create an original story woven around the mask characters using improvised dialogue. As a variation, the teacher may designate a familiar story or fairy tale (different one for each group) to be adapted to the mask characters in the groups.

19. Divide into groups of three. Each group forms a three-person creature, and arranges itself into the moving shape of the creature. Each person in the group then speaks five words relating to the creature, then four, then three, then two, and finally one last word. (Be prepared for some surprises as to creature choice (e.g., sloth, unicorn, octopus).

20. Read the poem "Jabberwocky" by Lewis Carroll. Define some of the unfamiliar words (e.g., brillig, slithy). Assign groups to play various parts as the poem is read by the teacher or other student, depending on grade level.

21. Plan a bank robbery in the old West executed by three inept bank robbers unaided by an equally unqualified stage coach driver.

22. Form a circle. Have each person say his/her name preceded by an adjective beginning with the same first letter as the name, while simultaneously using body movement, gesture, and voice described by the adjective (e.g., "tired Terry"). The class repeats the name and movements after each person speaks his/her name. The second person in the circle must then repeat the previous name and movement and add one of his/her own (e.g., "tired Terry, macho Michael," etc.). When the circle is completed, the entire group quickly repeats all of the names, one after the other in succession accompanied by appropriate gestures.

23. Divide into groups. Give each group a starting phrase (e.g., "This place scares me"). Have each group create a short scene based on the phrase line with dialogue and movement. Remind the groups that scenes must have a beginning, middle, and end.

24. Form groups of two. Create a *short* scene using the following dialogue. Add actions that tell the story.

A: Excuse me.

B: I beg your pardon.

A: May I?

B: What?

A: I believe that's mine.

B: I'm sorry.

A: Do you mind?

B: Of course not.

(Courtesy Dr. Joseph Juliano, Director of Fine Arts, Hamden CT. Public Schools)

The information on the preceding pages has contained little mention of the more "formal" side of drama—referring to the putting on of plays in which the children memorize their parts from a prepared script, rehearse, then play to an audience. While such productions may be time consuming, they offer abundant opportunities for children to gain valuable experience in the areas of acting, directing (to include blocking and casting), script writing, and scene design and other facets of theatre—all of which are cited as Content Standards for Theatre in the National Standards for the Arts.

Moreover, engaging in these experiences can foster other desirable learnings such as self discipline, working with others, perseverance, following directions, and more

Space does not allow the inclusion here of any complete plays; however, the authors has taken the liberty of including the following brief piece simply because it requires no extensive rehearsals and is fun to do. Note that the stage directions are part of the dialogue and intended to be read aloud by the actor. The source of this gem is unknown. As for its contribution to the field of drama, that is unknown as well.

The Fatal Quest

Characters: The King, the devoted Queen, the Duke, the Princess, the curtain. Directions: The lines are spoken as written, the characters including their stage directions as part of their speeches, at the same time suiting the action to the words.

I

Curtain: The curtain rises for the first act.

King: Enter the King.

Queen: Followed by the devoted Queen.

King: He seats himself on his throne, scepter in his hand.

Queen: The Queen stands gracefully beside him, gazing at him fondly. "My Lord," she says in gentle tones, "Why do we keep the Princess hidden from the eyes of men? Will wedlock never be hers?"

King: The King waxes stern. "Fairy Queen," he says gruffly, "a thousand times have I repeated—the Princess shall become the wife of no man."

Duke: Enter the handsome Duke. "O King," he says in manly tones, "I have this morning come from your majestic borders. I have a message of greatest importance."

King: "Speak," says the King with marked interest.

Princess: The Princess enters at the left. At the sight of the handsome Duke she is startled. Her embarrassment increases her loveliness.

Duke: At the first glance, the Duke falls madly in love.

King: The King rises in excitement. "Speak," he shouts at the Duke, "and be gone."

Duke: The Duke gazes at the Princess, his message forgotten.

Princess: The lovely maiden blushes and drops her eyes.

Queen: "Daughter," says the gentle Queen, "why do you intrude yourself here without permission?"

Princess: The Princess opens her mouth to speak.

Duke: The Duke holds his breath.

Princess: "Alas," says the maiden in tones melting with sweetness, "my angora kitten has strayed away and is lost."

Duke: "Fair Princess," cries the Duke in tones choked with feeling, "service for you were joy. The kitten I swear to find." With high courage he strides away.

King: "Stop him! Stop" shouts the King, fiercely. "My servants shall find the cat for the Princess." Exit the King.

Queen: Followed by the devoted Queen.

Curtain: The curtain falls.

II

Curtain: The curtain rises for the second act.

Princess: The fair Princess stands at the window. She hears the distant sound of hoofs. "It is he," she cries, placing her hand upon her beating heart.

King: Enter the King.

Queen: Followed by the devoted Queen.

Duke: The Duke steps in buoyantly, puss in arms.

Princess: "My kitten, my kitten," cries the Princess joyously. She takes her pet in her arms but her eyes follow the stalwart form of the Duke.

King: The King is pierced with jealousy.

Duke: The Duke falls upon his knees before the King. "O King," he says manfully, "I have found the kitten! I have come to claim the reward, the hand of the Princess."

King: The King trembles with wrath. "Begone," he shouts furiously. "The hand of the Princess shall be won by no cat."

Duke: The Duke departs. As he passes the Princess, he grasps her soft hand. "I will return," he whispers in her ear.

Princess: The Princess does not speak, but her clear blue eyes reflect the secret of her soul.

Curtain: The curtain falls.

III

Curtain: The curtain rises for the third and final act.

King: The King stands morosely in the center of the stage.

Queen: The Queen stands sadly beside him. "My Lord," she says in pleading tones, "relent. The Princess weeps day and night, nor will she be comforted."

King: The King turns his back. "Hold your peace!" he says in harsh tones.

Queen: The Queen weeps.

Duke: Enter the Duke, his sword at his side. "O King," he says in white passion, "for the last time I ask you for the hand of your daughter."

King: The King spurns him. "Begone," he shouts once more.

Duke: The Duke draws his sword and stabs the King.

King: The King gasps and dies.

Queen: "My Lord, my Lord," cries the Queen passionately, and she falls dead upon the King.

Duke: "Great Caesar's Ghost, what have I done!" cries the Duke in anguish. He drinks a cup of poison and falls dead.

Princess: Hearing the cry, the Princess enters. She stops transfixed at the horrible sight before her. "Heaven help me," she cries, waving her shapely arms. "I die of grief." She falls dead upon the breast of her beloved.

King: Woe, woe, the King is dead.

Queen: Alas, alas, the devoted Queen is dead.

Princess: The Princess is dead, and beautiful even in death.

Duke: The manly Duke is dead.

Curtain: The curtain falls forever.

Puppetry

Although we tend to associate puppetry with entertainment, its potential as an educational tool is even more significant. Spreading across all curriculum areas, puppetry's multiple benefits cover a broad spectrum, ranging from improving fine motor skills to more creative problem solving. In the process, strong emphasis on the senses is required, allowing sensory experiences to be recalled, processed, and re-created in a relevant form.

In the classroom, puppets can introduce new topics, impart information, and even exert a little discipline when appropriate. Educators in varied educational settings report using puppets to teach diverse topics ranging from algebra to dental hygiene, as well as folk music, history, poetry, and others.

Singularly significant, perhaps, is a puppet's power to remove the frequently perceived "wall" between child and adult that can sometimes obstruct learning. Playing the role of a nonthreatening, nonjudgmental "third person" on the scene, a puppet becomes a riskfree acceptable channel for releasing a child's fears, aggressions, and frustrations. Alleviated anxieties can result in greater self-confidence, an enhanced feeling of self-worth, and improved behavior on the part of the child.

Puppeteer/educator Judith O'Hare writes, "Puppetry offers children the ultimate disguise. . . . The puppet becomes an extension of the child, yet separate from the child. The puppet speaks loudly, forcefully, aggressively, angrily, kindly, etc. It offers the child anonymity and provides an imaginative environment for shaping and reshaping experiences and accumulated information into a dramatic presentation."[7]

Puppets also provide a comfortable vehicle for deepening empathy and understanding for those individuals challenged by physical, mental, or emotional impairments.

Jim Rose, son of famous puppeteer Rufus Rose (creator of Howdy Doody), rejects the notion that puppetry is only for children and an obscure part of the theatre. A professional puppeteer himself, Rose believes that looking at puppetry as child's play diminishes the importance of children, as well as the importance of puppetry as an ancient art—one that is still being practiced in many countries.

Puppets are classified in various ways—hand, rod, shadow, marionette, bunraku, and others—depending upon how they are manipulated. It is assumed that teachers will provide opportunities for children to learn about different types and experiment with creating them.

Simple forms of puppets may be made from a wide variety of materials including paper, fabric, wood, clay, wire, aluminum foil, socks/stockings, found objects, Styrofoam, cardboard, and more.

When storage space is available in the classroom, it is helpful to keep a supply of usable materials on hand—many of which can be obtained at no cost from local sources such as lumber dealers, department stores, and industrial firms. A starting collection might include:

- Wooden dowels and metal rods
- Foam rubber sponges
- Jewelry, buttons, ribbon, feathers, beads
- Used gloves
- Yarn
- Cardboard
- Plastic bottles/jugs
- Styrofoam balls
- Velcro
- Cardboard tubes from paper towels and bathroom tissue

- Packaging material
- Sticks of all kinds from various sources including doctor's offices (tongue depressors), paint stores (stirrers), and home (Popsicles)

A basic puppet theatre may be constructed from a large appliance box, lightweight fabric, and a portable light fixture.

The classifications shown below represent a small sample of some basic types of puppets. Teachers are urged to consult further references and web-sites (see p. 138) for a more complete view of puppetry.

Hand

1. A familiar type of hand puppet is made from an ordinary sock in which the hand is inserted into the toe and heel to form a movable mouth. As a variation, cut two pieces of mouth-shaped cardboard, tape together to form a hinge, and insert inside the sock to form a stiffer mouth. If preferred, colored felt may be glued to the cardboard, and then glue the cardboard to the outside of the sock in the heel/toe location. Use various objects to make facial features and other decorations as desired.

2. Insert hand into a lunch bag (or other paper bag), manipulate the folded section to note the position of the face, and then attach any appropriate objects to create features and clothing for a character of choice.

3. Finger puppets come to life when small cylinders are decorated with facial features and other adornments and worn on the fingers.

Shadow

Almost every country except the United States has shadow puppetry in its background. The first record of shadow puppets dates back to 120 B.C. in China.

Shadow puppets are back-lighted silhouettes attached to a stick, cardboard, or other similar material and manipulated with various devices ranging from simple handles to more flexible devices. A cotton sheet (upon which scenery may be painted if desired) serves as an improvised screen and is placed at right angles to a single 100-watt lamp used for the light source. Lacking the lamp, a handy overhead projector may be substituted. Shadow puppets grow larger when moved farther away from the screen.

Rod

Rod puppets may vary from the very simple (a decorated soda straw in a Styrofoam cup), to the more substantial, such as the following adapted from a creation by Judith O'Hare:

Materials include:

- 1 paper towel tube
- 5–6 pieces of newspaper

- Colored construction paper
- 1 large piece of colored tissue cut in half
- Scissors, glue/glue brushes, masking tape, markers

Procedure:

1. Tear 4–5 single sheets of newspaper; stuff lunch bag about one-third full. Add the paper towel tube and continue filling to a tight pack.

2. Tape bag to the tube with masking tape to secure and prevent wobbling of head.

3. Cut or tear pieces of construction paper to make features. Self stickers may be used.

4. For hair use one-half piece of the colored tissue. Fold in half, then fold in half again. Holding the folded end, cut from the bottom into $\frac{1}{4}$ to $\frac{1}{2}$-inch strips without cutting through the fold. Cut or tear at the fold to make two large pieces with strips. Spread glue on the bag where hair is desired and attach one section of strips, then the other to achieve a layered effect.

5. For body, use the other half piece of colored tissue. Circle the top of the neck tube below the chin area with glue. Gather the tissue and glue around the neck to hide the tube, making a simple costume. Leave a small opening at the back for the child's hand to grasp the tube.

Other creations classified as "puppets" by their creators include wooden spoons with facial features made from sticks, buttons, jewelry, and other objects, and dowels inserted in apples, oranges, and other edibles given faces with carrots, raisins, and celery.

In general, puppet heads are modifications of the basic cube, sphere, and oval shapes and may be made from Styrofoam balls, clay, balloons (inflated and covered with papier-mâché), pulp flower pots, milk cartons, stuffed stockings, plastic bottles, stuffed paper bags, and more.

Hair styles/beards/mustaches may be made from fake fur, fabric, yarn, embroidery thread, dyed string, mops, crepe paper, and tissue paper.

Characterizations are conveyed by appearance, voice, and movement. Children should be allowed to explore movements such as up/down, side to side, in a circle, and bending forward, as well as others that seem to fit the given puppet's character. It is suggested that they be allowed to experiment with different voices also.

Once the puppet is completed, have each child write a couplet (two lines that rhyme) that includes the puppet's name and some clue as to its character (e.g., "Goodness, gracious, mercy me. My name's Matilda Appleby," "Nippy's my name, I'm very neat. When you visit me, please wipe your feet," etc.).

Children enjoy telling more about their puppets—their likes/dislikes, history, hobbies, favorite expressions, favorite foods, and other vital statistics. Allow puppets to be asked questions by other puppets. Silly is fine. Some children are particularly fond of puppets that are not too bright.

Finally, have each child make a home for his/her puppet—a shoe box or some similar shelter is most acceptable, especially if the puppet's name is painted on the outside. If space allows, create a puppet condominium for living quarters.

— NATIONAL STANDARDS— GRADES K–4

Content Standards

1. Script writing by planning and recording improvisations based on personal experience and heritage, imagination, literature, and history.
2. Acting by assuming roles and interacting in improvisations.
3. Designing by visualizing and arranging environments for classroom dramatizations.
4. Directing by planning classroom dramatizations.
5. Researching by finding information to support classroom dramatizations.
6. Comparing and connecting art forms by describing theatre, dramatic media (such as film, television, and electronic media).
7. Analyzing and explaining personal preferences and constructing meanings from classroom dramatizations and from theatre, film, television, and electronic media productions.
8. Understanding context by recognizing the role of theatre, film, television, and electronic media in daily life.

Grades 5–8

1. Script writing by the creation of improvisations and scripted scenes based on personal experience and heritage, imagination, literature, and history.
2. Acting by developing basic acting skills to portray characters who interact in improvised and scripted scenes.
3. Designing by developing environments for improvised and scripted scenes.
4. Directing by organizing rehearsals for improvised and scripted scenes.
5. Researching by using cultural and historical information to support improvised and scripted scenes.
6. Comparing and incorporating art forms by analyzing methods of presentation and audience response for theatre, dramatic media (such as film, television and electronic media), and other art forms.
7. Analyzing, evaluating, and constructing meanings from improvised and scripted scenes and from theatre, film television, and electronic media productions.
8. Understanding context by analyzing the role of theatre, film, television, and electronic media in the community and in other cultures.

Source: Excerpted from *National Standards for Arts Education*, published by Music Educators National Conference (MENC). Copyright 1994 by MENC. Used by permission. The complete National Arts Standards and additional materials relating to the Standards are available from MENC—The National Association for Music Education, 1806 Robert Fulton Drive, Reston, VA 20191 (telephone 800-336-3768).

Content standards, as shown above, are intended to be achieved through providing opportunities for assuming various character roles, improvising dialogue, moving in different ways, directing dramatizations, working with technical elements (stage design, costumes, lighting, sound, etc.), writing original dramatic pieces (monologues, plays, skits, etc.), and exploring dramatic art in different settings such as television, film, and electronic media. Dramatic experiences involving other arts (music, dance, art, etc.) demonstrating their close relationship will also be included, as will dramatic arts from other cultures reflecting the universality of theatre.

— GLOSSARY —

Blocking: The designation of an actor's movements on stage.

Casting: The choosing of individuals to play certain characters in a dramatic production.

Creative drama: *Process-oriented* drama activities intended to enhance the social and emotional growth of an individual, as opposed to *product-based* dramatic projects intended mainly for performance.

Elements of drama: Speech, movement, intellect, imagination, senses, emotion, and others.

Improvisation: Unscripted, spontaneous dramatic presentation.

Kinesthetic: Related to position and body movement.

Mirror images: Partner activity in which one partner faces the other and "mirrors" his/her actions.

Pantomime: Acting without words, using only gesture, facial expression, and movement to communicate a message or express an idea.

Role-playing: Assuming the point of view of a designated character in a given situation and improvising appropriate dialogue, gestures, and speech to fit the role.

Senses: The pathways through which living creatures hear, see, smell, touch, and taste.

Scenery: Refers to items constructed for the stage to create the illusion of a given locale in a dramatic production.

Script: Playwright's written dramatic structure containing dialogue, movement directions, and other elements.

Tableau: Motionless human figures depicting a scene, idea, or theme without words or action.

Warm-up: Particular activities/exercises designed to prepare body and mind for involvement in drama.

— NOTES —

1. Brian Way, *Development Through Drama* (Amherst, NY: Humanity Books, An imprint of Prometheus Books, 1998).
2. Kahlil Gibran, *The Prophet* (New York: Alfred A. Knopf, 1951).
3. Frances Durland, *Creative Dramatics for Children* (Kent, OH: Kent State University Press, 1975).
4. Dorothy Thames Schwartz and Dorothy Aldrich (eds.), *Give Them Roots and Wings* (Washington, D.C.: American Theater Association, 1972).
5. Way, *Development Through Drama.*
6. Howard Gardner, *Frames of Mind* (New York: Basic Books, 1993).
7. Judith O'Hare, *You and Me Puppets* (74 Hillcrest Road, Reading, MA 01867. Tel: 781-944-0965; e-mail: jaohare@gis.net; and www.youand-mepuppets.com).

— FOR FURTHER READING —

Bernardi, Philip. *Improvisation Starters*. Cincinnati, OH: Betterway Books, 1992.

Bony-Winters, Lisa. *On Stage: Theatre Games and Activities for Kids*. Chicago: Chicago Review Press, 1997.

Booth, David. Story *Drama: Reading, Writing and Role Playing Across the Curriculum*. Markham, Ontario, Canada: Pembroke Publishing, 1999.

Cranston, Jeneral W. *Transformation Through Drama*. Trinidad, CA: Jenfred Press, 1995.

Heller, P. *Drama as a Way of Knowing*. York, ME: Stenhouse, Galef Institute 1995.

Jennings, Coleman. *Plays Children Love*. New York: St. Martin's Press, reprinted Jan. 1993.

Landy, Robert J. *Handbook of Educational Drama and Theatre*. Westport, CT: Greenwood Publishing Group, 1983.

Laughlin, M. K., and K. H. Lantrobe. *Reader's Theater for Children*. Englewood, CO: Teacher Ideas Press, 1990.

Lee, A. *A Handbook of Creative Dance and Drama*. Portsmouth, NH: Heinemann, 1985.

McCaslin, N. *Creative Drama in the Classroom*, 5th ed. New York: Longman, 1990.

Rooyackers, Paul. *Drama Games for Children*. Alameda, CA: Hunter House, 1987.

Scholastic Education. *The World of Theatre*. New York: Scholastic Inc., 1993.

Way, Brian. *Development Through Drama*. Amherst, NY: Humanity Books An imprint of Prometheus Books, 1967.

Warren, Bernie and Tim Dunne. *Drama Games*. North York, Ontario, Canada: Captus Press in association with MENCAP, 1989.

Puppetry

Baird, Bill. *The Art of the Puppet*. New York: Macmillan, 1965.

Champlin, Connie, and Nancy Renfro (illustrator). *Puppetry and Creative Dramatics in Storytelling*. Austin, TX: Nancy Renfro Studios, 1980.

Engler, Larry, and Carol Fijan. *Making Puppets Come Alive*. New York: Taplinger Publishing Co., 1972.

Hensen, Cheryl, and the Muppet Workshop. *The Muppet Puppets*. New York: Workman Publishing, 1994.

O'Hare, Judith. *Puppets: Education Magic*. You and Me Puppets, 74 Hillcrest Road, Reading, MA 01867; Tel: 781-944-0965; e-mail jaohare@gis.net.

Dance

> . . . dance is a part of human communication at its most fundamental level.[1]
>
> Dennis Sporre

Dance has played a significant role in human existence since the beginning of time. In primitive cultures, dance was among the instruments used to appease the gods in hope of gaining favors such as growing weather for crops, good health, fertility for humans and animals, and more. Dance also became one of the essential forms of response to events associated with such basic human experiences as birth, death, marriage, entry into adulthood, and others, including war—a virtual "kinetic human history" as one author termed it.[2]

In *Frames of Mind* Howard Gardner writes of "masked dancing, sorcerers and hunters depicted in the ancient caves of Europe and mountain ranges of South Africa," adding, "of all the human activities depicted in the caves, dancing is the second most prominent right after hunting. . . ."[3] Moreover, expression through dance is believed by some to have come before other classified forms of communication.

As for dance in education, there is evidence that it was used as a learning tool in the civilizations of Babylon and ancient Egypt to further the understanding of heavenly constellations. Also noted were the Greek philosophers who believed that dance was essential to balanced physical and mental development and recommended that it be a part of the education of all children. The Romans attempted to follow this example; however, like some of their other efforts, they missed the spirit of the Greeks. As a result, the character of dance in Rome plunged to the level of obscene and (as in mime) became forbidden by the church. (See p. 122.)

Along with other good things, the arrival of the Renaissance also heralded the return of the dance and its eventual designation as special art form. Classical **ballet**, in particular, is associated with the Renaissance because it had its beginnings in the court dances of Italy and France, rising to its highest point later in Russia.

FIGURE 6.1

BALLET POSITIONS

1st position—feet pointed out with
heels touching

2nd position—move right foot to the right
keeping feet apart and weight evenly
distributed on each foot

3rd position—touch heel of right foot
to arch in front of left foot

4th position—move right foot forward
slighty apart but in line with the arch
of the left foot

5th position—feet parallel opposites touching heel
of right foot in front of left toe and toe of right foot
in front of left heel

Ballet, as any child in a tutu can attest, is based on five positions, each of which prescribes the placement of the feet as well as the coordinated position of the arms. (See Figure 6.1.)

Narrative ballet is usually based on a story told through the movements of the dancers—each playing the part of a particular character (e.g., *The Nutcracker, Swan Lake, Sleeping Beauty*, etc.). **Abstract ballet** has no story, just a sequence of beautifully executed movements, sometimes associated with an idea. Positions in ballet are named in French (e.g., arabesque, plie, etc.), as are the particular presentations (e.g., *pas de deux*, dance for two; *pas de trois*, dance for three; etc.), and the chorus of dancers known as the *corps de ballet*.

The anti-balletic movement, known as **modern dance**, became most evident in the person of Isadora Duncan who claimed nature as her inspiration. Duncan advocated less prescription and more freedom in dance movement, stressed self-expression and fluidity, and was frequently known to improvise.

Of those who followed Isadora Duncan, perhaps the best known is Martha Graham, acclaimed for her **choreography** and execution of composer Aaron Copland's ballet *Appalachian Spring*.

Mention should also be made here of male dancer and choreographer Ted Shawn, who is credited with winning the right for men to dance. Before his time, dance was considered matriarchal. As a youth, Shawn had diphtheria and became paralyzed. Dance therapy was recommended—an event that changed the course of his life from divinity studies to dance. Shawn founded a company of male dancers and choreographed dances dealing mainly with traditional male orientations—sports, farm work, and war. He is also credited with founding Jacob's Pillow in western Massachusetts, which has since become the festival for international dance.

In addition to "modern dance," additional genres of dance have evolved over time, including ballroom, tap, jazz, country, break, theatre, and others, each of which can claim its own subclassifications.

Folk/ethnic **dances** are those that reflect particular cultures, and are usually executed to the traditional music of the country/people they represent. Like folk songs, their origins are frequently difficult to trace, having passed through generations without concern for authorship.

As many of us are aware, dance has come to be connected more with entertainment than with education—considered by many to be "nice" but not necessary—and its appearance in schools in any form ranges from "seldom" to "never."

More recently, the reported research of Howard Gardner and others, combined with the National Standards, have brought dance back to a respectable and rightful place in the curriculum, where with other arts, it can serve as a meaningful aesthetic experience as well as a viable learning mode.

Experiencing Dance in the Classroom

Like a violin in an orchestra, movement is the body's instrument of expression, engaging the emotions as well as the intellect—becoming the interpreter of feelings, sensory impressions, and ideas. Think on this:

We retain:

> Ten percent of what we read
> Twenty percent of what we hear
> Thirty percent of what we hear and see at the same time
> Fifty percent of what we hear, see and say
> Ninety percent of what we hear, see, say and DO.[4]

> B. Fauth

Appreciating the body as an expressive instrument comes about through exploration and discovery, which is what "creative movement" is all about.

Dance educator Margot Faught writes that creative dance provides "movement experiences that promote motor skill development and general body awareness, as well as basic learning skills such as listening, following directions, sequencing and problem solving."[5]

Eric Jensen reports that "dance can develop balance and ultimately reading skills,"[6] as revealed in his research related to the needs of a developing brain and the learning problems that can arise when such needs are not met. Jensen also notes that the "feel good chemicals" in the brain run higher after movement, which in turn can enhance learning and feelings of well-being.

In the classroom, movement/dance can elicit a sense of joy—a kind of "high" springing from a sudden awareness of greater confidence and elevated self-esteem—an inner exhilaration that shouts, "I feel good about myself!"

Dancer Martha Graham summed it up: "There is a vitality, a life force, an energy, a quickening that is translated through you into action, and because there is only one of you in all time, this expression is unique. . . ."[7]

Teachers who have never experienced the benefits of dance or tasted its delights in the classroom are urged to proceed without caution. There's plenty of help out there. (See pp. 158–160.)

ELEMENTS OF DANCE

Of all of the elements associated with dance, **body articulation** and *space* seem to lead the way in dance with children. Although *force*, **energy**, *intensity, time*, and others play a part, it is the movement of the body through space around which most activities revolve. When motivating movement with younger children, it is helpful to provide cues that will stimulate their thinking in terms of the context of a particular movement. The activities presented here include a few examples of such cues.

It is also suggested that movement/dance experiences be preceded by some form of **warm-up**. (See p. 121.)

LOCOMOTOR AND NON-LOCOMOTOR MOVEMENT

All dance is based on movement that may be classified as *locomotor* or *non-locomotor* (also known as **axial**).

Locomotor movement, sometimes called "traveling movement," takes the dancer somewhere. By means of walking, running, skipping, galloping, leaping, or jumping, children can transport themselves from one place to another. To perform **non-locomotor movements** such as stretching, bending swaying, reaching, and others, for the most part, children remain in place.

Space explorations may be expanded by varying locomotor and non-locomotor movements in different ways:

a. Changing the *direction* of the movement (forward, backward, in a circle, diagonally, etc.)
b. Changing the **level** of the body (high, medium, low)
c. Changing the *size* (range) of the movement (large, small, narrow, wide, etc.)

Focal points (objects/areas to which attention is directed) also play a role, along with **patterns** created by the movement of the feet over the floor.

Activities

1. Have each child feel his/her pulse and walk in the rhythm of the pulse beat.

2. Walk in different ways (e.g., like a robot, giant, giraffe, etc.).

3. Walk in ways that express different emotions (e.g., anger, happiness, etc.).

4. Walk through some imaginary environments (e.g., in space, through deep snow, on hot coals, in a cool stream, in a puddle of honey, etc.).

5. Walk the shapes of name initials, geometric figures, objects from nature, and others.

6. Discover ways to move from one place to another using two locomotor movements.

7. Using any desired accompaniment such as a steady drum beat played by the teacher, have the group walk four steps forward, four steps backward, four steps diagonally (specify which direction—left or right), then four steps in a circle in place (each person turning in his/her own circle).

Vary the foregoing walking pattern by adding each of the following (one at a time) on the *last count* of each direction:

a. Change the level of the body.
b. Add an arm movement with the change of level.
c. Add an arm movement and a vocal sound with the change of level.

8. For another variation on no. 7 above, add changes in tempo (fast/slow), foot position (flat footed, tip toe, high knee lifts), character (tired, full of joy), and more.

9. Form groups and have each group "choreograph" a 16-count (beat) movement composition that includes:

a. Locomotor and non-locomotor movements
b. Change of direction
c. Change of level

Inform children that if desired they may use different starting formations for their compositions (e.g., one line, two lines facing, a circle, or simply random spacing).

Other locomotor movements may be substituted for walking (e.g., *running* (in place, upstairs, against the wind, like a deer).

Note: For those children who are one-foot skippers, *skipping* may require a little assistance. Breaking it down to a *step-hop* on each foot and then gradually increasing the tempo may help to solve the problem.

Lots of things *hop* and *jump* (kangaroos, rabbits, frogs, and grasshoppers). *Leaping* involves "over" something, the cues for which can range from a narrow crack to a wide brook. Jumping rope, shoveling snow, raking leaves, and various occupations are additional possibilities.

Non-locomotor movements may also be varied through the use of cues:

- *Bending* (to pick up a coin, under the weight of a heavy backpack, etc.)
- *Swaying* (like a clock pendulum, like a tree in the wind—starting gently and increasing to a hurricane)
- *Stretching* (to paint a rainbow in the sky, like a rubber band, etc.)

Rhythm instruments are a valuable tool in movement—serving the teacher in many ways. For example, reducing spoken commands by acting as signals for (**a**) change of direction ("when you hear the triangle, walk backwards," (**b**) a change in body level, or (**c**) sudden stops in the action ("freeze when you hear the woodblock"). They may also be used to cue other movement changes, such as from locomotor to non-locomotor and more. On an added note, they serve well as a control device in the classroom to signal silence or simply a change of activity without the need for spoken cues.

a. Walk to the drum beat; skip when you hear the triangle.
b. Walk on tiptoe to the sound of the bells; stoop way down when you hear the cymbals.
c. Gallop to the sound of the sticks; march when you hear the drum.

Each locomotor movement has its own rhythmic pattern—walking is an *even* rhythm (♩ ♩ ♩ ♩); running is also an even rhythm but moves more quickly (♫♫). Skipping and galloping are both *uneven* rhythms (♪. ♪♪. ♪). (See p. 106.)

Awareness of the difference between even and uneven rhythms enables children to respond with the appropriate movements when the rhythms are sounded without spoken cues.

Combining these rhythms can produce various movement patterns:

♩   ♩   ♪   ♪   ♩

walk walk run run walk

Colored construction paper may also be used to designate a movement (e.g., red for walk, green for running, etc.; thus, two red papers placed side by side signifies two walking steps). As a reminder that running notes (♪ ♪) are executed more quickly than walking notes (♩ ♩), the green paper could be cut in half. Color may be coded to non-locomotor movements as well. By rearranging the colors, children can create their own movement compositions.

ACTION SONGS AND SINGING GAMES

Because the territory is familiar and the resulting comfort level high, action songs and singing games are a good beginning for the young. Moreover, they may serve as teaching tools (e.g., the familiar "Head Shoulders Knees and Toes," sung to the tune of "Here We Go Round the Mulberry Bush," designating parts of the body):

Head shoulders knees and toes (sing three times)

Clap   clap   bow

The tune "Tavern in the Town" is home to another frequently sung body song with more parts added:

Head shoulders knees and toes, knees and toes

Repeat

Eyes and ears and mouth and nose

Head shoulders knees and toes, knees and toes

A wiggle is added to the tune of "The Bear Went Over the Mountain":

a. My thumbs are starting to wiggle (sing three times)
   Around around around
b. My fingers are starting to wiggle, etc.

Repeat with hands, shoulders, head, feet (and more) ending with "Now all of me is a-wiggling" verse.

"One Two Three" (p. 77) is a slightly jazzier version; "Che Che Koolay" (p. 77) reminds us that learning parts of the body is pretty universal; even dinosaurs do it (p. 72).

Other familiar songs can serve the same purpose by simply adding appropriate verses.

"Let's Get the Rhythm" doesn't even require music—it's a chant, and may be done either in the manner of call and response (leader chants the first line, group repeats) or by having the whole group chant all the lines.

Let's Get the Rhythm

Leader: Let's get the rhythm with the head, ding dong (on words "ding dong" tip head from left to right)

Group: We've got the rhythm with the head, ding dong (repeat action as above)

Leader: Let's get the rhythm with the hands (clap clap)

Group: We've got the rhythm with the hands (clap clap)

Leader: Let's get the rhythm with the feet (stamp stamp)

Group: We've got the rhythm with the feet (stamp stamp)

Leader: Let's get the rhythm with the hips, hot dog! (on words "hot dog" swing hips from left to right)

Group: We've got the rhythm with the hips, hot dog! (repeat action as above)

All: Let's get the rhythm all together, ding dong (clap clap) (stamp stamp), hot dog! (All with actions as before).

When space is limited, the range of locomotor movements will be also. In the hope that no child will languish, the following may serve (use any music in $\frac{4}{4}$ meter):

1. Begin with four hand claps (one clap to each count)

- Add four foot taps
- Add four knee pats (using both hands at once)
- Add four finger snaps

Repeat the entire pattern a few times and then stop to ask for suggestions for other movements to add to make a sequence of eight different movements. To aid the group in remembering which movement comes next, have the individuals who make the suggestions cue the upcoming movement on the fourth beat of the preceding one (e.g., if head nodding is to follow finger snapping, then on the fourth finger snap the person who suggested it shouts "Head!"). If the group runs out of ideas, try these—touch shoulders, pat head, slap sides of thighs, swing hips, cross arms over chest, whistle, click tongue, march in place, and others—all four times each.

2. Pass the motion (use music in $\frac{2}{4}$ or $\frac{4}{4}$ meter for this activity.)

A circle formation is preferred; otherwise, have children stand at their places in such a way that all are visible to each other.

Teacher begins with two movements such as clap/pat and executes them to the music. The class joins in. The motion is then passed to the next child who retains either one of the teacher's motions but adds a different one for the second. All join in performing the child's two movements. Repeat with each succeeding child in turn. The cue for the movement to be passed to the next person is when everyone has joined in.

HAND JIVE[8]

Hand jive, as it is known, consists of a sequence of hand motions using music in moderate tempo. The following is set to music in $\frac{4}{4}$ or $\frac{2}{4}$ meter.

Clap, Snap and Tap[8]

Sequence 1

Clap hands	2 times
Pat knees	2 times
Pound right fist on top of left fist	2 times
Pound left fist on top of right fist	2 times
Hit right fist on palm of left hand	2 times
Hit left fist on palm of right hand	2 times
Bend left arm, touch left elbow with back of right hand	2 times
Bend right arm, touch right elbow with back of left hand	2 times

• Repeat the foregoing sequence until familiar, then add the following:

Sequence 2

Using right arm, swing a make-believe lasso over head in circular movement	4 times
Repeat lasso movement with left arm	4 times
Imitate a hitchhike motion with right arm, leaning body to the right	4 times
Imitate a hitchhike motion with left arm, leaning body to the left	4 times

Do a "cool wave":	
With palm facing out, make small circles at waist with the right hand, leaning body slightly back	4 times
Repeat circle movement with left hand	4 times
Make a victory sign (both hands clasped together over right shoulder)	2 times
Repeat victory sign over left shoulder	2 times
Reach right arm over head as if to catch a fly	1 count
Slap hands together	2 count
Do a throwaway motion with both hands	1 count
Stamp one foot	1 count

Thus, the four counts include reach, slap, throw, stamp (one count for each movement).

• Repeat the sequence until familiar and then combine with Sequence 1 (clap hands, pat knees, etc.) and repeat as many times as desired.

Divide the class into small groups of two each and perform the following sequence of movements to music in $\frac{3}{4}$ meter.

Waltz Tempo Patty Cake

Pat knees	6 counts (6 times)
Cross arms and touch shoulders	6 counts (6 times)
Clap hands	6 counts (6 times)
Clap partner's right hand	6 counts (6 times)

Clap partner's left hand   6 counts (6 times)
Clap partner's both hands   6 counts (6 times)

- When sequence is familiar, reduce movements to three each:

Pat knees   3 counts (3 times)
Cross arms and touch shoulders   3 counts (3 times)
                                                    etc.

- Then to one each:

Pat knees, touch shoulders, clap, etc.

- For variation, try reversing the sequence (e.g., clap partner's both hands, partner's left hand, partner's right hand, own hands, cross arms and touch shoulders, pat knees).
- Have children suggest their own hand jive motions to create more patterns.

Note: From *Clap, Snap and Tap*, CD Educational Activities Inc., Baldwin, New York. Used with permission.

CHAIR DANCING

Chair dancing is just that—dancing while sitting in a chair—so it is usable also in limited space.

By way of getting acquainted with this "art form" the movements suggested here are simple and easily executed by the young and the old. Have children create others.

Position: Sit up toward the front of the chair so that both feet are resting firmly on the floor and the body is in "good posture" position. If the classroom chairs have attached writing areas that cannot be moved, have children turn to the "open side."

Movements:

1. Extend right foot forward, tap heel on floor, and return to position.

       Count 1-2   Call "right back"

2. Repeat with left foot.

       Count 1-2   Call "left back"

3. Clap hands and hit right thigh with right hand.

       Count 1-2   Call "clap right"

4. Repeat clap and hit left thigh with left hand.

       Count 1-2   Call "clap left"

5. Punch the air with right fist two times.

       Count 1-2   Call "punch punch"

6. Repeat with left fist.

    Count 1-2   Call "punch punch"

7. Cross arms in front and pat both shoulders twice.

    Count 1-2   Call "pat pat"

8. Snap fingers of both hands two times.

    Count 1-2   Call "snap snap"

Repeat as many times as desired using any music in $\frac{2}{4}$ or $\frac{4}{4}$ meter with moderate tempo.

MUSIC AND MOVEMENT

"Do what the music tells you to do" is a phrase heard frequently in many classrooms. Unfortunately, to many children, the music tells them nothing because they have no movement repertoire with which to respond. In view of this, it is suggested that children experience some structured movement before being asked to engage in "free expression"—the justification being that a basic store of knowledge upon which to draw can increase the possibility of more satisfying creations. Providing children with such "equipment" will help to enrich their future efforts and conceivably yield more worthy outcomes.

It seems pertinent to note here that what a teacher considers "appropriate response" to music played may not always be what is forthcoming from the children; thus, be prepared for surprises. Emma Sheehy writes of a classroom experience in which the very "slow walking" music being played was interpreted by one boy as "fast running," which he proceeded to do. When asked by a classmate, "Don't you hear the music?" his reply was, "Yep, but it don't bother me none!"[9]

MOTIVATING CREATIVE MOVEMENT

Music is a loving companion to movement but not always a necessary one. In the area of creative movement, for example, some types of music may serve only to elicit movements that children have observed through the various media and, in the process, produce predictable results and restrict the flow of creative ideas.

If a teacher wishes to use music to motivate creative movement, it is suggested that it be in a less familiar form such as a solo flute, oboe, cello, or other orchestral instrument recorded or played by a guest artist or older student. Rhythm instruments, various types of drums, and other percussion are also possibilities. Additional sound sources for movement may include vocal sounds, environmental sounds (natural and other), poetry, psalms, and stories.

Creative movement may also be inspired in more "nontraditional" ways—through the feel of various textures and shapes, smells of various foods, perfumes, greenery, etc., as well as through viewing paintings, designs, abstract symbols, sculpture, and other forms of art.

Finally, in movement as in all other arts, for inspiration we need only to turn to the wellspring of all creativity—the senses.

Interpreting Musical Terms through Movement

Tempo is a musical term referring to the speed of the music. Select a movement of choice. Perform it very slowly and then very fast.

Dynamics include the loud and soft places in the music as well as the climaxes. Select a movement. Execute it very gently and then with maximum force.

Crescendo means gradually growing louder, whereas *diminuendo* means gradually growing softer. These two terms may be shown in movement by starting at a low-level body position, rising as the music grows gradually louder, at the same time increasing the size of the movement, and then returning to original position while gradually decreasing the size of the movement as the diminuendo occurs in the music. If suitable music is not available, use the crescendos and diminuendos on a drum, cymbal, or tambourine.

Pitch refers to the highness or lowness of the sound. For a high pitch, stretch the body for full length and gradually descend as pitch becomes lower. Lowest pitch should coincide with lowest level body position.

Melodic contour is determined by the sequence of pitches as they occur in a given piece of music. Some melodies go up and down, some down and up; others go both ways, take wide leaps, or hover closely around a few selected notes. In this activity, it is intended that body movement be such that it describes the contour of the melody. Contour may also be expressed using hand and arm motions only.

Form has several meanings in music. When referring to the design created by repetitions and contracts, such as ABA/form, for example, similar movements are repeated on the A sections and different movements executed on the contrasting (B) sections of the music.

ACCENT, METER, AND RHYTHM

When the upper figure of the time signature is 4, the meter moves in 4, with the accented beat falling on the first beat of every 4. When the upper figure of the time signature is 3, the meter moves in 3, with the accented beat falling on the first beat of every 3. To reenforce the feeling for accent and various meters, try the following:

- Have each group perform one movement on the first beat and a different movement on the remaining beats of any given meter. For example, in a group of four, the movements might be:

CLAP	SNAP	SNAP	SNAP
1	2	3	4

or

PAT	CLAP	CLAP	CLAP
1	2	3	4

In groups of three, the movements might be:

STAMP	CLAP	CLAP
1	2	3

or

SNAP	PAT	PAT	(knees)
1	2	3	

As the group warms up, vary the activity by pointing to any member of the group who must then immediately change the movements, keeping the first movement different from the others in order to emphasize the accented beat. The group executes the new movements until another person is cued by the leader to introduce new movements. Use music in any meter desired. Tempo should be moderate.

The contrast between musical terms such as *staccato* and *legato* may also be shown through executing contrasting percussive and sustained movements. Have the group originate their own ways of reenforcing the meanings of various musical terms by examining a list of such terms and then choosing several for this purpose. If the group is large, divide into small groups and have each group select one term to perform for others to identify.

INSTRUMENTS OF THE ORCHESTRA

When children have become familiar with various instruments of the orchestra, form class into groups of two or three and ask the following questions:

"If any given instrument of the orchestra could walk by itself around this room how might it move? Do you think the sound it makes might influence its way of moving?

Direct groups to choose any instrument they wish to depict, then move in its manner. Have other groups identify the instrument.

Dances

The dances shown below are representative of what may be termed American folk dance. They are included here because they easily are learned and may be accompanied by singing if recordings are unavailable. (See Resources pp. 159–160.)

Music:	"Yankee Doodle"
Formation:	Random scattered
Verse:	Yankee Doodle went to town a-riding on a pony
	Stuck a feather in his cap and called it Macaroni
Actions for Verse:	March in place 16 steps.
Chorus:	Yankee Doodle keep it up, Yankee Doodle dandy
	Mind the music and the step and with the girls be handy
Actions for Chorus:	Clap 6 claps (one to each measure) followed by 4 claps in rapid succession.

Music:	"Shoo Fly"
Formation:	Circle of Partners (ladies on right of gentlemen)
Verse:	Shoo Fly don't bother me (Sing 3 times)
	For I belong to somebody
Actions for Verse:	With hands joined, walk into center of circle raising hands up over head, then backward out of the circle lowering hands. Repeat in and back.
Chorus:	I feel I feel I feel I feel like a morning star
	I feel I feel I feel I feel like a morning star
Actions for Chorus:	Face partner. Hook right elbows and swing 8 counts. On second line of chorus hook left elbows and swing 8 counts.
	Gentlemen may move on to new partner here if desired.
	Repeat from beginning.

Music:	"Oh, Susanna"
Formation:	Single circle, ladies on gents' right.
Words:	I come from Alabama with my banjo on my knee
Action:	All ladies walk four steps toward the center of the circle and four steps back to place. (Walking back should be done without turning around.)
Words:	I'm going to Louisiana, my true love for to see.
Action:	All gents walk four steps forward and four steps backward.
Words:	It rained all night the day I left,
	The weather it was dry,
	The sun so hot I froze to death,
	Susanna, don't you cry.

Action:	Grand right and left as follows:
	Partners face each other and join right hands. They move forward, passing right shoulders with each other, then drop right hands and extend the left hand to the oncoming person, pass left shoulders, drop left hand, extend right hand to the oncoming person, etc. Direction should always be forward—do not turn around when taking hands. The ladies move clockwise around the circle, and the gents counterclockwise, weaving in and out.
Words:	Oh, Susanna, oh don't you cry for me
Action:	On the word "cry," each gent takes the nearest lady for his new partner, and swings all the way around once.
Words:	For I come from Alabama with my banjo on my knee.
Action:	Partners cross hands, skating fashion, and promenade (walk) around the circle counterclockwise. The gents are on the inside, and the ladies on the outside. Continue promenading with partner until the word "knee" is sung. Repeat entire song and action as often as desired.
Music:	"Bunny Hop"
Formation:	Single line with hands on the waist of person in front.
	Kick left foot out to the left and hop on the right foot at the same time.
	Repeat.
	Kick right foot to the right and hop on the left foot at the same time.
	Repeat.
	Jump forward on both feet.
	Jump backward on both feet.
	Three jumps in place on both feet.
	Repeat from beginning.

SQUARE DANCING

Square dancing is a joyous, upbeat activity in which all ages may participate; thus, it is not surprising that in recent years the number of groups devoted to square dancing has proliferated to the point where nearly every city or town has at least one group meeting regularly to dance together for the sheer fun of it.

Because of the wealth of recordings and instructional materials available, no attempt will be made here to explore the whole field in depth but rather simply to introduce some basic terms, to provide directions for a few dances (some needing only singing accompaniment).

For additional information see "Resources," pp. 159–160.

SQUARE DANCE TERMS

SET	Four couples in a square formation, ladies on right of gentlemen
HEAD COUPLE	Couple closest to the music and/or caller
SIDE COUPLE	Couple to the right and left of head couple
PARTNERS	Those standing side by side
CORNERS	Those standing at right angles

BASIC CALLS

HONOR YOUR PARTNER	Bow to partner
HONOR YOUR CORNER	Bow to corner
CIRCLE RIGHT	All join hands and circle to the right
CIRCLE LEFT	All join hands and circle to the left
FORWARD AND BACK	Move forward to greet approaching person, make a quick bow or curtsey and return to place (walking backwards)
DO-SI-DO YOUR PARTNER	Face partner with arms in folded position at shoulder height. Move forward, passing partner on right and then return to place without turning around.
DO-SI-DO YOUR CORNER	Face corner and execute same as with partner (above).
ALLEMANDE LEFT YOUR CORNER	Extend left hand to corner person and turn completely around once, returning to place.
GRAND RIGHT AND LEFT	Face partner, extend right hand to grasp partner's hand. Move *forward*, passing partner on right, extend left hand to oncoming person. Continue walking *forward*, alternating right and left hands until back to original position.
	Note: When introducing grand right and left for the first time, caution group to always *walk forward*—never turn around—when alternating left and right hands.
PROMENADE	Standing side by side partners assume skating position (left hand joined in

partner's left, right hand joined in partner's right) and walk in a counterclockwise direction around the circle.

SONGS FOR SQUARE DANCING

Music:

"Hinky Dinky Parlez-Vous" using words below, which describe actions.

Formation:

Square of four couples, ladies on gents' right.

Words:

1. Head two ladies go forward and back, parlez-vous
Forward again and do-si-do, parlez-vous
Do-si-do with your corners all and do the same with your own little doll, hinky dinky parlez-vous.
2. Side two ladies go forward and back, parlez-vous
Forward again and do-si-do, parlez-vous
Do-si-do with your corners all and do the same with your own little doll, hinky dinky parlez-vous.
3. Head two gents go forward and back, parlez-vous
Forward again and do-si-do, parlez-vous
Do-si-do with your corners all and do the same with your own little doll, hinky dinky parlez-vous.
4. Side two gents go forward and back, parlez-vous
Forward again and do-si-do, parlez-vous
Do-si-do with your corners all and do the same with your own little doll, hinky dinky parlez-vous.

Note: When children are familiar with the above directions, a slightly more advanced version may be tried substituting the following calls for those beginning "Do-si-do with your corners all" etc:

Allemande left with your corners all
Grand right and left around the hall
hinky dinky etc.

— NATIONAL STANDARDS —
GRADES K–8

Content Standards

1. Identifying and demonstrating movement elements and skills in performing dance
2. Understanding choreographic principles, processes, and structures
3. Understanding dance as a way to create and communicate meaning
4. Applying and demonstrating critical and creative thinking skills in dance
5. Demonstrating and understanding dance in various cultures and historical periods
6. Making connections between dance and healthful living
7. Making connections between dance and other disciplines

Source: Excerpted from *National Standards for Arts Education*, published by Music Educators National Conference (MENC). Copyright 1994 by MENC. Used by permission. The complete National Arts Standards and additional materials relating to the Standards are available from MENC—The National Association for Music Education, 1806 Robert Fulton Drive, Reston, VA 20191 (telephone 800-336-3768).

Content standards, as shown above, are designed to be achieved through experiences related to the elements of dance, involving such areas as locomotor/ non-locomotor movement and variations, responding to meter in music, improvising, sequencing/patterns, choreographing original dance compositions, performing dances of different cultures, and discovering ways of reenforcing learnings in related arts and other subjects through dance.

— GLOSSARY —

Abstract ballet: Ballet based on an idea as opposed to that based on a story (narrative ballet) with emphasis on skillful execution of prescribed ballet movements.

Axial movement: See *Non-locomotor movement.*

Ballet: Genre of dance originating with court dances of Italy and France. Based on five positions and prescribed movements named in French (e.g., *plie*).

Body articulation: Movement of the whole body and/or parts of the body through space.

Chair dancing: Dancing while sitting in a chair using various movements executed from a seated position.

Choreography: The act of creating a dance, including the selection of steps, directions/arrangement of movement, and other components.

Elements of dance: Space, time, force, intensity, body articulation.

Energy: The amount of stress applied to a movement.

Focal point: Object or area upon which the eye is focused.

Folk dance: Dance growing out of a particular culture and executed to its traditional music. Passed down through generations.

Form: Structure or design of a dance composition.

Genre: Category or classification of dance, that is, ballet, jazz, folk, and so on.

Gesture: A movement by the hand or other part of the body to communicate an idea or emotion.

Hand jive: Sequence of movements executed mainly with the arms and hands.

Level: Height of the body as it relates to the floor (e.g., standing = high level; kneeling = low level).

Locomotor movement: Movement that takes the body from one place to another (e.g., running, walking, skipping, etc.). Sometimes referred to as "traveling" movement.

Modern dance: Genre of dance less prescriptive than ballet, emphasizing more self-expression and freer movement. Associated with Isadora Duncan and later, Martha Graham.

Narrative ballet: Ballet based on a story in which dancers assume character roles.

Non-locomotor movement: Movement performed while remaining in one place (e.g., stretching, bending, swaying, etc.).

Patterns: Figures created by movement of feet over the floor in the course of a dance or exercise.

Range: Refers to the size of a movement (e.g., small/large, wide/narrow, etc.).

Square dance: Dance in which couples are arranged in a square formation.

Tempo: Rate of speed at which movement is performed.

Time: An element through which movement is organized.

Variation: Any alteration applied to a given movement while at the same time allowing the movement to retain its basic character.

Warm-up: Particular movements/exercises designed to prepare the body and mind for involvement in dance.

— Notes —

1. Dennis Sporre, *Perceiving the Arts* (Prentice Hall Inc., A Simon and Schuster Company, 1992).

2. Hanna Judith Lynne, *To Dance is Human*: *A Theory of Non-Verbal Communication* (Chicago and London: University of Chicago Press, 1987).

3. Howard Gardner, *Frames of Mind*, 2nd ed. (New York: Basic Books, 1993).

4. B. Fauth, "Linking the Visual Arts with Drama, Movement and Dance for the Young Child." In *Moving and Learning for the Young Child* ed. W. J. Stinson. (Reston, VA: American Alliance for Health, Physical Education, Recreation and Dance, 1990).

5. Margot Faught, "Creative Dance for All Abilities." In *Early Childhood Creative Arts*, Proceedings of the International Early Childhood Creative Arts Conference—Lynnette Overby, Senior Editor; Ann Richardson and Lillian S. Hasko, Assistant Editors; Luke Kahlich, Managing Editor. National Dance Association, an association of the American Alliance for Health, Physical Education, Recreation and Dance, 1991.

6. Eric Jensen, *Arts with the Brain in Mind* (Alexandria, VA: Association for Supervision and Curriculum Development, 2001).

7. From an interview.

8. Used by permission of Educational Activities Inc., P. O. Box 87, Baldwin, NY 11510 Phone 1-800-645-3739 e-mail: learn@edact.com

9. Emma Sheehy, *Children Discover Music and Dance* (New York: Henry Holt, 1959).

— FOR FURTHER READING —

Brown, J. M. (ed.). *Graham 1937: The Vision of Modern Dance*. Princeton: University Press, 1979.

Choksy, Lois, and David Brummit. *101 Singing Games and Dances for Elementary Schools*. Upper Saddle River, NJ: Prentice Hall, 1987.

DeMille, Agnes. *Speak to Me, Dance with Me*. Boston: Little Brown, 1973.

Downey, V. "Expressing Ideas Through Gesture, Time and Space." *The Journal of Physical Education, Recreation and Dance* (1995).

Fleming, Gladys Andres. *Children's Dance*. Reston, VA: National Dance Association, 1990.

Gilvern, Anne Green. *Creative Dance for All Ages*. Reston, VA: NDA AAHPERD, 1992.

Griss, Susan. *Creative Movement: A Language for Learning Educational Leadership*, no. 5 (1989): 75–80.

Highwater, Jamake. *Dance: Rituals of Experience*. New York: Alfred Van der Marck, 1978.

Kassing, Gayle, and Danielle Jay. *Dance Teaching Methods and Curriculum Design*. Champaign, IL: Human Kinetics, 2003.

Kassing, Gayle, and Danielle M. Jay. *Teaching Beginning Ballet Technique*. Reston, VA: National Dance Association, 1998.

Klosty, James. *Merce Cunningham*. New York: E. P. Dutton, 1975.

Murray, Ruth Lovell. *Dance in Elementary Education*. New York: Harper's, 1978.

Pica, Rae. *Moving and Learning Across the Curriculum*. Albany, NY: Delmar, 1999.

_____. *Experiences in Movement*. Beltsville, MD: Gryphon House, 2001.

_____. *Experiences in Movement*. 3rd ed. Albany, NY: Delmar, 2004.

Pomer, Janice. *Perpetual Motion: Creative Movement Exercises for Dance and Dramatic Arts*. Champaign, IL: Human Kinetics, 2002.

Smith-Autard, Jacqueline. *The Art of Dance in Education*. London: *A & C Black*, 1998.

Stinson, Due. *Dance for Young Children: Finding the Magic in Movement*. Reston, VA: National Dance Association, 1988.

Thompson, Myra K. *Jump for Joy* (Creative Movement Activities for Young Children). Parker Publishing, 1993.

Weikert, Phyllis. *Teaching Movement & Dance: Intermediate Folk Dances* High Scope Press, 1989. (Accompanying recordings available).

— RESOURCES —

Dances We Dance, Vita Richardson, 3795 Canterbury Lane, STE. 177 Bellingham, WA 98225 2000. (Recordings, video, teachers' guides available.)

Multicultural Folk Dances, Vols. 1 & 2, Susan Langhout and Christy Lane, Human Kinetics 1998 (CDs/Cassettes/Videos).

Square and Folk Dances: Complete guide for students, teachers and callers Hank Greene, Harper & Row, 1984.

Human Kinetics, P. O. Box 5076, Champaign, Ill 61825-5076
e-mail: orders@hkusa.com.
Tel: 1-800-747-4457

— VIDEOS —

From Teacher's Video
Choreography by Balanchine
Dance Theatre of Harlem
Dancing—8 videos on History of Dance
Denishawn: Modern Dance
He Makes Me Feel Like Dancin'
Merce Cunningham
Tribute to Alvin Ailey

From Kimbo (Recordings and Guide)
All Time Favorite Dances
Circle Dances for Today
Dances in a Line

From Educational Activities Inc.
  1937 Grand Ave. Baldwin, New York
  1-800-645-3739
  e-mail: learn@edact.com
  website: www.edact.com
  (Recordings and Guide)
  Get Ready to Square Dance
  Square Dancing for All Ages

Human Kinetics, P. O. Box 5076, Champaign, Ill 61825-5076
  e-mail: orders@hkusa.com
  Tel: 1-800-747-4457

PART III

Integrating the Arts

7

Making Connections

It is not arts education that we do, it is . . . life education.[1]

The materials presented on the following pages represent only a sample of what might be considered "connections" between the arts and other classroom disciplines. Although previous chapters relating to each of the arts contain activities involving other subject areas, it was felt that bringing a number of these suggestions together under the headings of other classroom disciplines might be helpful.

Themes provide a broad umbrella under which to relate all areas of the curriculum, enabling learning to be achieved through varied pathways. They may be short term, such as those based on a holiday, special event, or something as simple as a song, yet remain launchings for journeys into many different areas.

Although topics such as "The Sea," "Seasons," and others can spawn a myriad of activities in all disciplines, it is the less "targetable" ones such as "Respect," "Friendship," "Time," "Cooperation," and even "Greed" that may prove the more challenging.

As most teachers are aware, some subject areas are more "fertile" than others and as such, offer more possibilities for integration. The materials presented here are included simply by way of identifying a few possible pathways to what is hoped will be pleasure as well as enhanced learning.

Relationships between seemingly unrelated things are not always perceived by some individuals. The story is told of a high school student who was having a problem with a word in English class and sought help from the English teacher. Her admonition to him was "You should know the meaning of this word, you had it in Latin," to which the student replied, "Yes, but that was across the hall."

Lots of things are "across the hall" to individuals who have difficulty making connections. Encouraging learners to examine elements and conditions to discern possible relationships in contrasting settings could conceivably contribute to the development of their own creative potential as well as to exciting new discoveries in the future.

In the process lies the hope that among the following, teachers will find activities appropriate for their own classes, modifying and adapting as desired to suit the needs of particular grade levels. The assumption here is that children and teachers alike will initiate ideas of their own that will prove far more creative than any of those offered—which is really what this book is about.

Social Studies

The broad range of subjects included in any given social studies curriculum can offer opportunities for abundant arts connections, particularly in those areas related to various cultures, including our own. The activities suggested below are intended to increase student involvement as well as enhance desired learnings.

1. Create a collage representing a particular era or event in history.

2. View a painting depicting an historical event, study all the elements closely, and bring the painting to life through dialogue, sound, and movement.

3. Construct simple puppets representing historical figures of choice and then improvise a discussion between selected figures on a topic of their time. Using the same figures, discuss a contemporary issue in terms of how it might be handled from their individual points of view.

4. Observe and listen carefully to the sights/sounds in your household or neighborhood, then try to describe them in musical terms such as pitch, tempo, dynamics, harmony, timbre, and others. Compare the morning and evening scene in the same terms.

5. Explore the arts contributions of various ethnic groups in selected regions of the United States. Check local museums for additional information.

6. Divide into groups. Direct each group to choose a legend, fairy tale, holiday, historical or other event they wish to commemorate in a "living" sculpture and then arrange themselves in appropriate positions to depict the subject. (Allow planning time.)

7. Explore the origin of various folk instruments of the world, focusing on geographical location, accessibility of materials, occasions on which they were used, and who played them.

8. Divide into groups and direct each group to depict a household appliance of 1776 in movement only (no sound) and then a modern household appliance for others to identify.

9. Learn folk songs and singing games from around the world and compare with familiar ones in the United States. Execute some simple folk/ethnic dances of selected world cultures. (See pp. 152–153.)

10. Listen to large musical works reflecting nationalism (e.g., those depicting historical events, memorializing heroes, using patriotic themes, national anthems, folk tunes, etc.).

11. Explore works of art that depict the descriptive characteristics of a particular region of the United States and/or the time period in which they were created.

12. Bring in various types of hats that clearly define occupations and/or characters (e.g., fireman's helmet, bonnet, hard hat, etc.). Have children choose parts to play. Create a situation and then improvise dialogue that ensures a beginning, middle, and end. Discuss ways in which these different occupations interact with each other.

13. Research the origin of folk, national, and familiar melodies found in large musical works e.g., *The Moldau* (Smetana), *1812 Overture* (Tchaikovsky), *Billy the Kid* (Copland), and *American Salute* (Gould).

14. Send some messages through drums as African drummers do. Station students around the room to represent villages. Through the use of certain combinations of drum beats and various drums, send a message from the first drummer to the second who in turn relays it to the third, etc.

15. Form groups. Select a nursery rhyme, fairy tale, or fable. Identify the problems encountered by the characters and work out solutions. Dramatize.

16. Research some of the work songs used in various occupations (sailing, mining, laying railroads, etc.). Sing while pantomiming the task for which they were intended.

Note: Work songs served not only to ease the strain and monotony of the job but also to unify the group effort for greater productivity. Some songs even contained hints about working conditions, e.g., *Drill Ye Tarriers* sung by railroad workers (Grade 5 The Music Connection Series, Silver Burdett Ginn).

17. Explore the influences of lifestyles on the type of dances performed in various countries (e.g., are dances more vigorous in cold countries?).

18. Research the history of dance in America. Discover possible relationships and influences of particular types of popular music on dance.

19. Discover and learn songs of the world that reflect universal human emotions (e.g., love, sorrow, joy, etc.).

20. Role-play familiar greeting styles and then research ways of greeting in different cultures.

21. During the study of lives and times of historical figures, have children choose favorite personages they wish to portray and then prepare short skits containing facts about their human side as well as their role in history.

22. Write a poem or compose a song about the state in which you live. Feature famous places and other information. As a follow-up, design a brochure intended for advertising your state to attract more visitors.

23. Explore examples of music, art, drama, and dance that reflect changes in the culture of the United States.

24. Select an historic event in U.S. history (e.g., American Revolution) and then improvise dialogue between some of its figures (e.g., American commander, British general, and a drummer or fifer) presenting their views on the event.

25. Create Japanese "mon" or family crests that symbolize yourself and your family.

26. View the sun symbols observed in early drawings up to the present and then create a personal sun symbol reflecting your heritage and facets of your personality.

27. Assume the role of a famous person you admire and then create a monologue that includes glimpses into the person's early life, failures, successes, contributions, and other items of interest. Biographies are a great source of interest for creative plays.

28. a. Research the history of the United States as revealed through its song, then compose one based on a contemporary event. Songs can not only reveal historical facts but also can provide clues as to the collective feelings of people involved in a country's events, for example the civil rights movement and anti-war and other protests.

   b. United States history is also represented in its poetry. Repeat the activity above substituting poetry for music.

29. Listen to and sing some of the songs born of war (e.g., American Revolution, Civil War, War of 1812, World War I, World War II, etc.). It is interesting to note that there are many more songs about war than about peace.

In this connection it may be of interest to learn that the tune of the "Star Spangled Banner" is based on an old British drinking song and that the tune of "America" is the same as England's "God Save the Queen."

30. Form groups. Have each group create a new country. Include:

   a. Name of country
   b. Motto
   c. Favorite food
   d. Favorite sport
   e. Favorite greeting
   f. Predominant form of transportation
   g. Flag (design in color)
   h. National anthem (compose)

Mythical/magical kingdoms cheerfully accepted.

Note: Allow ample planning time for these groups.

Science

Wondering is the beginning of science.[2]

Close observation of objects plays a major part in science as does different ways of looking; thus, an "awareness walk" comes at the top of the arts and science integration list.

1. Take an "awareness walk," observing closely shape, texture, line, and color of leaves, rocks, trees, shells (if beach), and other objects in the natural environment. Gather an assortment and create a collage, mobile, or sculpture from the objects.

Note: When available, new computer-adaptable microscopes enable children to look at things collected from their walk in even greater detail; also the use of a digital camera can help them think about observing from different angles.

2. Show the growing cycle of a seed in movement having various children assume the roles of necessary natural elements such as sun, rain, and wind. (With young children the words "The farmer plants his seeds" may be sung to the tune of "Farmer in the Dell." Succeeding verses include "the wind begins to blow," "the rain begins to fall," etc., sung as parts are played).

3. Create in movement a representation of how large fires can erupt from small sparks, with one or two children playing the part of the small sparks and others the surrounding elements that become ignited and eventually destroyed.

4. Sing songs related to environmental concerns, such as "Flowers Won't Grow" (see p. 79).
   Create new verses to familiar tunes or create new songs about saving the environment.

5. Interpret through movement the stages leading to the birth of a butterfly.

6. Listen to large musical works containing sections depicting natural phenomena (e.g., "The Planets" (Holst), "The Four Seasons" (Vivaldi), "And God Created Great Whales" (Hovhannes), "Aviary" (Saint-Saëns), "Morning" (Grieg), "Clair de Lune" (Debussy), "Grand Canyon Suite" (Grofé).

7. Play recorded sounds from different environments (sea, rain, forest, etc.) for the class to identify.
   Form groups. Using vocal sounds only, have each group create a sound of the environment for others to identify. (See p. 65.)

8. Walk in the appropriate manner in various designated environments (space—no gravity; under water—resistance, etc.) hot pavement, cool grass, mud, and others.

9. Create a "sound collage" in different ways, using:

   a. "Found" instruments (see pp. 86–87)
   b. Recording of different sounds
   c. Sounds produced from objects in the immediate environment (desks, walls, machines, etc.)

10. Discover different parts of the body and different ways of using the body as a percussion instrument to produce different sounds (see p. 65).

11. Relate sound to the construction of various musical instruments in terms of vibrations, air columns, and different effects produced by various kinds of striking, blowing or plucking.

Explore reasons for using certain kinds of wood for the manufacture of certain orchestral instruments such as strings, some woodwinds, and selected percussion.

Make some "found" instruments (see p. 86).

12. Draw objects as they appear when viewed through a magnifying glass or a microscope.

13. In groups of two, pantomime motions involved in using various tools, with one person playing the part of the tool, the other person the operator (e.g., screw/screw driver; tire/air pump, etc.). Have others identify the action.

14. Identify a need for some new tool, object, or process that would facilitate some facet of daily living. Draw it, write about it, and/or show it in movement.

15. Build a "people machine" with moving parts and sounds. Start with one person assuming a desired position and moving some part of the body while accompanying the movement with an appropriate vocal sound. Have others join one at a time to become parts of the machine, using different movements and sounds. If space is limited, divide the class into two groups. Assign each person in Group A a counterpart in Group B. As individuals in Group A assume their positions, instruct counterparts to observe closely so that they may assume the same positions when the machine is "dismantled" and "rebuilt."

16. Build a human clock (position children on floor with clock numbers and hands). Show different times through change of positions. Form bodies in shapes of numbers and Roman numerals.

Explore the sounds made by different kinds of clocks including those with striking mechanisms.

Move like pendulums in various clocks, noting differences in speed of the swing depending on the length of the pendulum.

17. Represent a thermometer in movement and then improvise a conversation between Centigrade and Fahrenheit.

18. Create a dance composition based on the properties of a magnet.

19. Improvise a dialogue between:

matter and energy
earth and an object orbiting it
sea creatures reflecting on their needs, environment, impacting sources, and concerns

20. Feel your pulse and walk to its beat and then express the beat through a movement of choice. (Increase the intensity of the movement and note changes in the pulse beat.)

21. Explore the meaning of the word *rhythm* and then identify evidence of rhythm in the universe (day-night, tides, seasons, etc.). Compare to rhythm in music and art (see pp. 104 and 105).

22. Draw different phases of the moon.

23. Interpret an atom in movement.

24. Explore ways of depicting the circulatory system in movement. Do the same with the solar system.

25. Create movement representing forces that shape the features of the earth (e.g., water, etc.).

26. Choreograph a dance portraying a solid, a liquid, and a gas and the changes brought about when they interact.

27. Have groups of children assume roles of endangered species and improvise dialogue reflecting their lifestyles, habitats, and concerns.

28. Imagine being in some unfamiliar distant place (e.g., North Pole, bottom of the sea). Using improvised dialogue, dramatize a scene revealing conditions, inhabitants, perceived problems, and possible solutions when applicable.

29. Explore the possibilities ("What could happen if _____") of something presently existing in the world, changing, or disappearing and then improvise a dialogue representing the reactions of those affected.

30. Portray four elements (earth, air, water, fire), interpreting in movement changes in their forms when mixed with each other and/or with the addition of another, such as the moon, cold/hot, and more.

31. Create body movement representing the different forms that water can become under various conditions and during transitional stages from one form to another. If desired, form groups and then assign each group a particular form for others to identify.

32. Dramatize the energy chain, adding appropriate movement.

33. In the following, dramatize the roles played by:

a. Various organisms in living systems
b. Parts of electrical circuitry

34. Choose a favorite scientist, explore his or her background, and then create a monologue including selected events of childhood, successes, failures, inventions, and other facts. A few simple props and clothing appropriate for the period can add interest.

35. Form groups. Have each group conceive its version of how the birth of a given invention might have come about. Prepare a short skit to present. (Humor is always welcome.)

36. Dramatize a food chain (pyramid) with improvised dialogue describing the nature of the creature and its relationship to those preceding or following it in the progression.

37. Explore the connections between a country and its plants. Form groups. Have each group choose the plant it wishes to portray in a given country and then create a presentation that communicates the nature of the plant and its contribution to the environment.

A brief final word: Much was written in previous chapters about the importance of refining our sensory equipment, and this certainly applies to science as well as other areas. The references were, of course, to the five senses that are well understood and accepted. It is the question of the "sixth" sense that frequently disturbs scientists when they are confronted with inquiries about its existence because some facts are proven, others debatable. In this connection, mention is frequently made of the exceptional sensory powers of animals such as sonar in dolphins, infrared vision of snakes, magnetic detection systems of birds, bees, and others, as well as the ability of various sea creatures to sense electric fields. More recently, there are reports that dogs can predict an oncoming epileptic seizure, flare-up of fibromyalgia, heart attack, and other conditions in humans before they happen. To date there seem to be no well-defined answers. As Harvard University neurologist Steven Schachter put it, "Whatever it is, I think there's something to it."[3] (And that's not too skeptical for a scientist.) It would seem that this might be a topic of interest to upper-level students. (Its connection with the arts will have to come later.)

Mathematics

At a recent meeting of a group of elementary mathematics leaders in Montana one of them said:

> I wish all elementary school teachers could realize how much mathematics they are teaching when they are not teaching the mathematics lesson. So many connections could be made between mathematics and the other subjects.[4]

It is hoped that some of the "connections" about which this teacher spoke may be found among the following suggested activities.

1. Create a collage based on a math concept or a favorite number.

2. Use numbers, shapes, and colors for tone-matching games in early grades (see p. 71).

3. Create songs and raps for learning various math concepts, days, and months. If preferred, set words to a familiar tune. Use rhythm instrument(s) of choice to accompany raps.

4. Form angles and different line segments in body movement.

5. Play songs on the harmonica from numbers (see p. 89).

6. Sing the song "Two in the Middle" (see p. 75) and then add new verses with more numbers and/or subtracting numbers.

7. Using the tune "Here We Go 'round the Mulberry Bush," write the shapes of numbers as described in the following verses:[5]

    a. You start at the top and then go down (sing three times)
       To make the numeral one (1).
    b. Halfway round and then straight out (sing three times)
       To make the numeral two (2).
    c. Halfway round and halfway round (sing three times)
       To make the numeral three (3).
    d. Down and out and then right down (sing three times)
       To make the numeral four (4).
    e. Back and down and halfway round (sing three times)
       To make the numeral five (5).
    f. You go straight down and then around (sing three times)
       To make the numeral six (6).
    g. You go straight out and then straight down (sing three times)
       To make the numeral seven (7).
    h. You make an S and go up straight (sing three times)
       To make the numeral eight (8).
    i. You go around and then straight down (sing three times)
       To make the numeral nine (9).
    j. You go straight down, then all the way round (sing three times)
       To make the numeral ten (10).

8. Illustrate concepts of size (S, M, L) with younger children by having them make snowmen using three Styrofoam balls in graduated sizes glued together and adorned with buttons/beads for eyes, pipe cleaners for arms, and other accessories if desired. As a variation use different colored pom-poms in place of balls. Decorate as desired with ribbon, feathers, fabric, and other items to create a creature of choice.

9. Sing counting songs in various languages. Add rhythm instruments (p. 82), dramatization and movement where applicable.

10. Explore many different ways to create a circle—stationary or in motion—using different parts of the body.

11. Create pictures from tangrams.

12. Research how sculptors used techniques of addition and subtraction to create their sculpture figures. (See Art p. 40.)

13. Write a favorite number in the air to musical accompaniment using various parts of the body (e.g., finger, hand, forearm, both arms, head, torso, etc.), increasing the size of the movement to correspond with the body part used. Use gentle, nonobtrusive music in a slow tempo so that movements may be executed slowly—not necessarily in rhythmic response to the music.

14. Form a circle, to musical accompaniment; walk in a clockwise direction eight steps (counts), raise arm on the count of 2, and clap on the count of 4 reverse direction on count of 8. Repeat as many times as desired.

15. Make shapes of numbers with the body, using two persons to make a two-digit number and/or perform other functions such as addition and subtraction.

16. Create a human abacus or computer. Add sounds.

17. Fill eight same-size soda bottles with measured levels of water to produce notes of a major scale. Number bottles 1 through 8—low Do to high Do. Write out number sequence for various songs and play. (See p. 88.)

18. Starting on middle C of a keyboard instrument, assign a number (from 1–8) on eight neighboring white keys and then choose a random number sequence and play. If desired, add some words. As a variation on the foregoing, find a telephone number containing only the numbers 1 through 8 and play as before.

19. Use Cuisenaire rods to show the mathematical relationship of note values in music, using the longest rod for the whole note and adapting others. The point to be made is that regardless of the meter signature, the mathematical relationship between various kinds of notes remains the same no matter what party is in power. For example, a whole note is equal to two half notes; a half note is equal to two quarter notes; a quarter note is equal to two eighth notes, etc. See the diagram below.

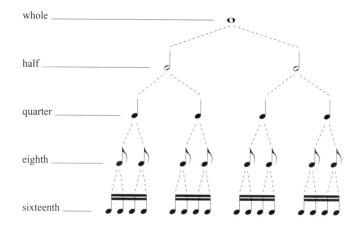

20. Execute conducting patterns to music in different meters. (See p. 105.)

21. Create a melodic percussion instrument from lengths of pipe measured for specific pitches. (See p. 92.)

22. Play a rhythm instrument orchestration.

23. Form groups and create geometric shapes and forms for others to identify. (See Art p. 42.)

24. Using geometric shape as a theme, draw or paint a version of theme and variations on the selected shape.

25. Perform line dances, circle dances, and square dances (see pp. 152–155).

26. Relate instruments of the orchestra to sets and subsets in mathematics (see p. 93).

27. Relate seriation in mathmatics to:
  a. patterns in art (see p. 40)
  b. note values or pitch levels of a scale in music (see p. 103)
  c. patterns in movement and dance (see pp. 142–149)

28. Describe various geometric shapes in locomotor movement and then in non-locomotor movement (see p. 142).

29. Create different designs on a Geoboard.

30. Discover patterns represented in various musical forms (see p. 64).

31. Explore computer music and art.

32. Research contributions of Pythagoras and Newton to music and art.

33. Make personal clocks using plastic lids from dairy containers or other suitable source. Glue on numbers or write them with markers. Make long and short hands from twist ties and fasten them with a paper fastener. Use to learn time or designate beginning times for other scheduled classroom activities.

34. Construct a three-dimensional object (cube, pyramid, etc.) from soda straws, connected by pipe cleaners.

35. Make rubbings from coins. Explore other textured surfaces suitable for this activity. (See p. 50.)

36. Show artworks by artists (e.g., Mondrian's *Broadway Boogie Woogie*) that focus solely on the arrangement of elements such as space, shape, color, and line. Have children create their own versions of this type of art. Show also examples of Cubist art (Picasso and others) in which the subject matter is reduced to geometric forms.

37. Discover the rhythm in such vocabulary words as pentagon, octagon, vertex and others, sound it in some form, and then create movement to it.

38. Explore various movements that can represent symbols of time duration (e.g., clap while saying "one-a-thousand" to time a second).

39. Express quantitative concepts in movement (e.g., large, small, long, short, light, heavy, etc.) by varying the size, character, or other quality (see p. 143).

40. Draw a human figure using the following measurements related to body proportions. (It is interesting to note in this connection that despite our differences, we all seem to have common body proportions.) When drawing a human form, each body part is drawn in proportion to all the others:

Body Proportions[6]

   a. The height of a person's head is about one-seventh the height of the whole body.

   b. The size of the hand usually equals the distance from the chin to where the hair begins.

   c. The length of a foot equals the height of the head.

   d. The length of an arm and hand equals half the height of the body from the shoulders to the ground.

   e. The hips come halfway between the top of the head and the ground.

   f. The upper and lower parts of the arms are equal in length.

   g. The knee comes halfway up the leg.

41. Try a *grand march* for counting 2s, 4s, and 8s. This activity requires a large space.

   a. Line up children (one behind the other) in two parallel lines facing the front.

   b. When the music begins, the leader of one line turns left and marches to the rear; the leader of the other line turns right and marches to the rear at the same time.

   c. At the rear, both lines meet and walk forward in twos.

   d. As the couples reach the front of the room area, one couple goes left, the next right, and so on, alternating down the line.

   e. As couples meet at the rear, they walk forward in fours to the front of the room. End people pivot in place as each line marches around in a circle to the left, to form equidistant lines moving like spokes of a wheel.

   f. Close up to make four lines again, marching in place, and then march forward. At the front, one set of four goes left, one goes right, alternating down the line. At rear, the fours meet to form lines of eight and march forward.

42. Create a design made from overlapping geometric shapes cut from construction paper. Experiment with different arrangements of the shapes, then attach to paper or other surface to complete.

43. Create a mobile using only numbers or shapes.

44. Design a park and make a map of it using different symbols to depict locations.

45. Design activities in music, movement, drama, and art that will illustrate in various ways the meaning of the word "opposite."

Language Arts

1. View a painting or other artwork and then write a poem or story inspired by the work.

2. Heighten the dramatic effects in a favorite poem or story through the use of rhythm instruments, allowing learners to discover:

    a. Places where a sound effect would enhance the reading (e.g., to portray a character, increase suspense, etc.)

    b. Which instrument best produces the desired sound

    c. Manner in which the instrument should be played (e.g., tambourine shaken or rapped) (see p. 82)

3. Discover ways of making shapes of letters with the body and then divide into groups to spell words for others to identify.

4. Write initials in the air using different parts of the body, beginning with small finger movements, and then progressing to larger movements using whole hand, forearm, both arms, head, torso. Accompany with music, fitting the character of the movement to the music heard (e.g., flowing, "angular," etc.).

5. Form a circle. The teacher starts a story using a very brief introduction (as brief as "Once upon a . . .) and passes it on to the first child in the circle who continues with the story until a prearranged signal is heard to pass it along. The signal may be in any form desired (e.g., sound of a triangle, tambourine shake, etc.).

    Variation: A ball of yarn with colors connected at selected places may be prepared. The first person in the circle starts the story while unwinding the yarn slowly and must continue until that particular color is all unwound, and then the ball is passed on to the next person who continues with the story until that color is used up, and so forth.

6. Discover many things that can be done with a name:

    a. Say it a different way (e.g., in another voice, whisper, emphasis on a different syllable, loud/soft, sad/joyful, repeated like a chant, etc.).

    b. Sound the rhythm of it using a rhythm instrument, clapping, tapping feet or in other ways.

    c. Dance to it.

    d. Write it in any desired shape across a full sheet of paper using all the space.

    e. Discover how to say it in another language.

    f. Research its origin.

    g. Find other words in it and/or think of as many words as possible beginning with each of its letters.

    h. Write it in the air to music (see No. 4 above).

    i. Make a blooper or spoonerism out of it.

    j. Create a collage and/or a mobile using the name letters.

7. Write the following words in ways that will communicate their meaning and/or their sound:

SPATTER   CRACK   EXPLODE   POWER   SIZZLE   CRESCENDO

8. Create some new words to familiar tunes that will help to achieve the desired learning, as in the following poem related to vowels composed by two college students:

THREE BLIND MICE

One short vowel (repeat) (hold up one finger.)
All alone, (repeat) (cross arms in a hugging motion.)
But he doesn't actually seem to mind, (shake head.)
If you look all around him you're sure to find (shade eyes, look around.)
At least one consonant right behind (Thumbs over the shoulders.)
That one short vowel! (Hold up one finger.)

Kathy Johnson and Kathy Fiese
SCSU Graduate Students/Classroom Teachers

9. Select a favorite poem, and then:

  a. Capture its essence through any form of artwork (painting, sculpture, etc.).
  b. Interpret it through creative movement.

10. Have some fun with spoonerisms (bloopers). Make up some new ones. "Prinderella and the Cince" is a classic. Memorable excerpts from it include "shirty doors" (dirty chores), "beep her kizzy" (keep her busy), "slopped her dripper" (dropped her slipper), and "sisty uglers" (ugly sisters).

11. Look up some old adages and give them new endings (e.g., "It's always darkest_____," (such as, "before pitch black"); "You can lead a horse to water_____"; etc.).

12. Relate meter in poetry to meter in music (see p. 105).

13. Discover many ways to say "goodbye" and "hello" in our language and others. Form groups and assign each group either one of the words. Each group is to create its own interpretations of the word using a variety of ways (e.g., dramatic presentation, music/songs, poetry, dance, etc.).

14. Update a fairy tale, nursery rhyme, fable, or legend, bringing it into this century. (See Drama, Chapter 5.)

15. Make a mobile of favorite book characters.

16. Create puppets based on book characters and perform the story.

17. Give each child a different letter and a square of felt to decorate. Decoration should illustrate a word beginning with the designated letter. When completed, all squares can be mounted on cloth to create a wall hanging.

18. Create a sound story and then divide into groups, assigning each group a sound to be made when certain words are read. (Sound sources may be vocal, clapping, stamping, rhythm instruments, or other.)

19. Relate choral speaking to music, citing commonalities such as voice production, pitch, dynamics, tempo, interpretation, and others. Create a choral speaking composition selecting solos, duets, and more. Have a student conduct the work.

20. Discover references to musical instruments and/or dances in literature of various periods.

21. Write some original words to familiar tunes to serve an occasion/event or activity.

22. Set some familiar poems to music.

23. Compose a short opera, operetta, or a play with music.

24. Have each child create a rebus (word picture) based on a term related to any of the arts.

25. Following familiarity with instruments of the orchestra, discuss which might be appropriate for portraying selected characters in a favorite story or other literature.

26. Study the words of the most frequently sung U.S. patriotic songs ("Star Spangled Banner," "America," "America the Beautiful") to understand more clearly their meaning and then interpret in the following ways:

    a. Tableau
    b. Creative movement/dance
    c. Dramatization

27. Read some poems for two voices. (See Fleischman, *Joyful Noise: Poems for Two Voices*, p. 186.) Form groups of two and have each group compose one to perform for class.

28. Dramatize or dance the following highlights excerpted from the story "Trying on Turtle's Sandals":[7]

Turtle is proud of her speedy hoofs
Deer admires her antlers in a stream, but is sad about her claws, which prevent her from moving quickly.
Turtle moves from place to place.
Deer is curious about how Turtle moves so quickly; she feels jealous and thinks up a plan.
Turtle is resting.
Deer approaches Turtle with a "good morning" greeting.
She asks: "What's up?"
Pretending to notice Turtle's hoofs for the first time, Deer asks if she could try them on.
Turtle is pleased by the attention, but she refuses to lend her hoofs to Deer.

Deer pleads with her.
Turtle still refuses.
Deer begs Turtle.
Feeling selfish, Turtle unclips her hoofs and gives them to Deer.
Putting on the hoofs quickly, Deer runs like fire!
She disappears!!
Turtle waits sadly for Deer to return. She waits some more.
Finally, Turtle puts on Deer's claws and walks slowly away.
Deer runs like fire and wind!
Crawling ever so slowly, Turtle turns her head to listen—and waits.*

(Story told by Arawak Indians who live in the rain forests of Guyana—formerly British Guiana.)

29. Create dance or movement that will communicate the spirit of the following poem:

MIST[8]

Whenever the wind
Blows off the sea
To throw herself
In the arms of me,
And press cool mist
Against my cheek—
 I cannot speak.

 Vilate Raile

30. Read Mary O'Neill's book *Hailstones and Halibut Bones* and then have children create poems about their favorite colors.

31. Discover terms common to poetry and music, such as accent, meter, phrase, rhythm, and others.

32. Write a cheer for a favorite team and create appropriate movement for it.

33. Form groups. Assign a word to each group to interpret in tableau (see p. 42) for others to identify (e.g., triumph, defeat, please, etc.).

34. Stimulate creative writing through music listening experiences in any one of the following ways:

 a. Describing scenes brought to mind by the music
 b. Creating an original story or play inspired by the music
 c. Creating a poem inspired by the music

35. Listen to selected symphonic musical works based on children's literature (e.g., Cinderella, The Three Bears) and other descriptive/program music. Create an original dramatization or interpret with puppets constructed for the purpose (see p. 131).

36. Record a sequence of different natural and man-made environmental sounds for identification by the class (e.g., surf, wind, ball bouncing, whales, traffic, etc.) and then have each child create an original narrative incorporating the sound heard. Children could also improvise a short skit based on the sound sequence. The following piece was written by a student in response to this assignment in a college undergraduate course. It is included here because it represents an example of looking at things in different ways—a point frequently referred to in this book:

> Pablo the popcorn kernel stayed perfectly still. He was very uncomfortable squashed next to all of the other popcorn kernels and a bit scared. He sat patiently in the bowl, listening to the steady, rhythmic ticking of the timer. **TICK TICK TICK TICK** . . . Pablo felt a warm breeze—a steady wind that sounded as if a strong, powerful fan was blowing. Some of the other kernels began to shift around uncomfortably in the microwave, and the wind seemed to howl louder. Suddenly, Pablo heard a loud **POP!** Like the sound of a ping-pong ball flying back and forth, the popcorn kernels popped one after the other—**POP POP POP POP** . . . Pablo felt a rumbling deep inside him like rolling thunder. It got louder and louder until it sounded like a booming growl—and then—**B O O M ! !** Pablo flew up into the air and seemed to burst with tremendous energy. He felt as light as a feather and gently swooshed downwards onto a fluffy cushion of white popcorn. Pablo liked his new look; he was light, and bright, and had a much more interesting shape now. **DING! DING!** A bell rang. The wind stopped blowing and the clock stopped ticking. Pablo, in his bowl, was placed on a high table. He didn't know what to expect next. And then, he saw a huge, crashing wave headed towards him. Plunging through the popcorn and drenching everything in its path, the waves of butter came tumbling over Pablo, sounding like one loud, roaring explosion after another. Then, Pablo heard a soft tapping, which quickened to a fast clapping. It got louder and faster as a storm of salt rained down onto the popcorn. A few round, white crystal salt-flakes landed right on Pablo and stuck to him. Finally, things quieted down again. Pablo smiled with content; he was happy with what he had become—a yummy piece of popcorn.
>
> Allison Cohen

37. Learn to "sign" a favorite song or poem.

38. Write a "rap" on a nursery rhyme, fable, legend, fairy tale, or favorite topic and perform, using selected rhythm instruments to maintain tempo and pulse. The following example is a beginning of a rap on the "Tortoise and the Hare."

> Hey brother Tortoise, hey brother Hare
> Hows about a race to the county fair
> Brother Hare laughed a big ho ho
> Race with you? What a way to go
> I'll be so far ahead in this thing
> You won't make it till half past spring,
>
> etc.
>
> (RPG)

39. Write a script for a film or videotape, then create a story board (sketches of scenes coordinated with accompanying dialogue), film it, and select appropriate background music to accompany the work.

40. Create a dialogue between two instruments of the orchestra relating clues as to their appearance, sound, origin, and manner of playing.

41. Pass an object around to spark ideas for a story in which the object will play a part (coin, key, etc). Do the same using a sound made by teacher (loud banging, rapping on desk, footsteps, squeaky door). Recorded sounds such as a train whistle may also be used. Children should have their eyes closed when the sounds are made by the teacher.

42. Create some original poems in the following forms:

  a. Haiku
  b. Tanka
  c. Cinquain
  d. Diamonte
  e. Eight line
  f. Spatial

(See pp. 180–183.)

Poetry

Great poems should be felt in the throat, the solar plexus and down the spine.

A. E. Houseman

Just after sunrise on the Big Springs Ranch in northeastern Nevada, saddle leather creaked, spurs jingled, coyotes yipped. Then one more sound of the West was heard—a cowboy reciting poetry.

Mike Nichols, Universal Press Syndicate

The foregoing appeared in a news account covering the tenth annual Cowboy Poetry Gathering in Elko, Nevada (one of a one hundred and fifty such gatherings held throughout the year) where readings by the cowboys evoked a gamut of emotions (laughter to tears) from the audience.

A recent pilot program of poetry initiated in a state prison became the vehicle not only for prisoners' therapeutic venting but also for discovery of talent in unexpected places.

The foregoing examples were included here as a reminder that poetry is not confined to poets and schools; rather, like its related arts, it is a universal form of expression.

Poetry's alliance with the arts is such a close one that it seems appropriate to include a brief summary of some of the forms that lend themselves well to arts interpretations. As most teachers know, these forms do not depend on rhyming schemes. *Haiku*, a form of Japanese verse dating back to the seventeenth century expresses a single idea, usually pertaining to nature, and is most frequently written in the present tense.

line one	5 syllables
line two	7 syllables
line three	5 syllables

Try setting a piece of Haiku to tones of the pentatonic (5 tone) scale, using the black keys on a keyboard instrument as the five tones. Number them 1 to 5 beginning with the three black (1-2-3) followed by the two black (4-5). Place the Haiku where it may be viewed by the class and ask them to call out a number (from 1 to 5) for each word. Write the number over the corresponding word and then play the melodic sequence of numbers (one line at a time) as shown, for children to evaluate. Upon hearing the completed melody they may wish to make alterations. If desired, invite suggestions for adding rhythm to the melodic sequence. The nature of Haiku is such that children may be content with little rhythmic variation.

Tanka (from the Japanese word *tan*, meaning short, and *ka*, meaning verse) consists of 31 syllables divided as follows:

line one	5 syllables
line two	7 syllables
line three	5 syllables
line four	7 syllables
line five	7 syllables

Like Haiku, Tanka is also about nature, with feelings of yearning added.

Cinquain, invented by an American poet, consists of five lines, each with a designated number and type of word:

line one	1 word—noun (subject)
line two	2 words—descriptive adjectives
line three	3 words—action verbs related to subject
line four	4 words—relating feeling about the subject (may be short sentence or four separate words)
line five	1 word—synonym or one capturing the essence of the poem (essence preferred)

When written as indicated above, the shape of the poem is similar to that of a Christmas tree.

Diamante poetry is somewhat akin to Cinquain; however, its diamond shape (from its name) is well defined when written in the accepted form. Diamante deals with *two contrasting* subjects, introduced to each other in the fourth line.

line one	1 noun (subject #1)
line two	2 descriptive adjectives for subject #1
line three	3 action verbs related to subject #1
line four	4 nouns (first two related to subject #1, second two related to subject #2)
line five	3 action verbs relating to subject #2
line six	2 descriptive adjectives for subject #2
line seven	1 noun (subject #2)

Eight line form consists of eight lines in which the last word of each line must be the beginning word of the next line. The final eighth line should bring unity to the whole poem.

Concrete or *spatial* verse refers to poems that are written in the shape of the subject of the poem. For example, a poem about angels might be created in the shape of wings or other object traditionally associated with angelic portrayal.

The following poem was written by a classroom teacher of 12-year-old children who knew them very well. Create some movement that reflects its content.

ON BEING TWELVE[9]

Twelve is a ball
That bounces high,
Twelve is a whistle
Haunting the sky.

Twelve is a rocket
Flushed to a dream—
Plying a hammer
Or stitching a seam.

Twelve is a bud
Straining to burst,
Twelve is a desert
Sighing with thirst.

Twelve is a pocket
Cluttered with things,
Twelve is a promise
Spreading its wings

      Anna R. Maskel

By way of rounding out the topic of connections, the following were excerpted from comments made by a group of in-service teachers—representing various grade levels and subject areas—as part of a sharing session in a recent university graduate course. Their ideas, comments, and supporting testimonials are included here because it was thought they might be of interest to other educators.

1. "Social studies has provided students with an opportunity to choose from and complete independent learning activities that address several of the Multiple Intelligences identified by Howard Gardner. For example, after an in-depth study on the Mayas, Incas and Aztecs, students were able to choose between activities such as: write a song based on a Mayan myth, re-create temples or buildings used by the Incas, write an editorial for or against human sacrifice, research and explain how modern math would be different had the Mayas not discovered the number zero. . . ."

2. "While teaching a social studies unit on ancient Egypt . . . some of the art-based projects were:

- Mummifying a wooden spoon
- Creating and decorating a tomb and mask
- Designing and coloring a new scarab beetle
- Ancient Egyptian cloth, jewelry and pottery making
- Mural of the Nile River showing the crops that grow
- Creating a new Sphinx that symbolized you (head of human, body of animal)
- Making a flail and crook and discussing their symbolism
- Poem/story about King Tut
- Making a new crown of Egypt
- Acting out the Pharaohs' decision to combine Upper and Lower Egypt
- Building a pyramid
- Measuring objects in cubits
- Making a name cartouche with hieroglyphics."

3. A fourth-grade teacher reports on "the culmination of a unit of study on China in which the children made an artifact for the China museum based on their research. They learned traditional Chinese songs and practiced the art of brush painting. . . . In other classes children wrote scripts for Reader's Theatre based on traditional Chinese folktales and performed them." This teacher also reported creating museum displays demonstrating some aspect of the children's research on the Arctic, as well as making dioramas, masks, and murals.

4. "When studying Australia, we discussed Aboriginal art, then made a giant mural of Aboriginal art . . . then writing about the picture or making art projects like a gingerbread house. . . . We have also done Native American symbol paintings on crumpled paper bags to simulate tree bark paintings. When reading an African tale, we made an African mask. When studying reptiles we did a lot of art. We made models of them, colored chameleons to show camouflage and colors to show their feelings. . . . we have made dioramas to show a child's favorite scene from a book. We have also done different kinds of poetry like acrostics and Tanka poetry. We recently did a Tanka poem about what a kite might feel like in the air, then we made paper bag kites. . . . Recently we made believe we were survivors from the Titanic . . . taking turns interviewing each other. . . . When we study Ireland I show an Irish dance video 'Riverdance.' We have sung songs for rhyming, phonemic awareness and word families . . . also made hero quilts and women's history quilts."

5. "Our fourth-grade class worked on a six-week unit on Egypt culminating in an authentic Egyptian burial . . . involving research and cooperative learning in the areas of history, science, visual and language arts, dance and linguistic performance. The entire school worked on a cooperative weaving project focusing on diversity . . . the process served as inspiration for writing. It also gave older students the opportunity to teach.

6. An art teacher reports on some of the ways that she has "brought the disciplines together."

   a. The use of music and movement to develop drawing skills and retention of art vocabulary in the primary grades.
   b. Creating clay ant hills with a first-grade class.
   c. Working closely with the media specialist to develop lessons for grades 3–5 that tied historical movements and artist biographies to their artistic style.
   d. Working with a third-grade teacher to develop a parallel between the creation of a visual and written story, using Edward Hopper's artwork as inspiration.
   e. Reinforcing third-grade study of Native Americans we studied Pueblo culture and created traditionally styled clay storytellers . . . also researched the many functions of totem poles and created totems that would represent their families.
   f. Working on art projects that complemented their study of animals and their habitats, fourth graders created a series of endangered species prints, inspired by Warhol. . . . they also invented their own animal caricatures, personifying certain characteristics. Relying on their newfound knowledge of weights and balances, the children sculpted papier-mâché wobbly head animals.
   g. Fifth-grade students were inspired to do a creative writing piece after they drew a symbolic representation of themselves.
   h. Students wove their own baskets in order to better understand one aspect of how Colonial Americans lived. They also created covered wagons filled with supplies to learn how people traveled west."

". . . during the reading lessons, the children break into groups to create story retells . . . when the children must retell the story in any manner they choose. Some draw the story in story frames . . . others create mini plays to act them out."

7. An eighth-grade teacher reports that "while the class was reading *Romeo and Juliet*, pairs of students were assigned to research geography, music, and costumes of the times"; in art they made their own masks for the ball scene in the play. Swords were also made in art ". . . it became a very integrated experience for the students and many graduates upon return to visit always comment on how much they learned while reading, acting, creating art, performing and putting the whole thing together. . . . One other year instead of *Romeo and Juliet* for literature we read fairy tales . . . we chose three tales, divided up the class (of 30) into three groups, split those into defense and prosecution and held trials on Goldilocks, the wolf from the three little pigs, and Jack from the beanstalk . . . students wrote their own dialogue and acted out the three trials for the whole school with music they had chosen and costumes . . . two boys who did not wish to act on stage video recorded the play. . . ."

8. An eighth-grade learning disabilities teacher, ". . . I co-teach with the reading and language arts teacher on our team. As part of our curriculum . . . students participate in Reader's Theatre and in mini productions of plays in the classroom. We teach a unit on poetry and read and write our own works. The students are encouraged to respond to literature with a variety of visual or oral representations. Eighth-grade students are very creative when given the opportunity to express themselves in ways that would be considered 'non-traditional.' "

9. From a seventh-grade teacher, "I never thought of singing in social studies before. I could look for folk songs from the states and countries we study . . . and songs like "Happy Birthday" in other languages . . . then create instruments native to the country under study. . . ."

10. "Once a week my class participates in an Artists/Writers Workshop. The students receive their inspiration for writing a creative story from a particular artwork, an illustrated story or a piece of music chosen by the teacher. After one of these art forms is discussed, the students then draw a picture while listening to classical music . . . followed by putting themselves 'inside their picture' and creating an original story. We then have an 'Artists/Writers Share' during which time the pictures are displayed and the stories read."

11. "In reading, for part of the year, my class is involved in Literature Circles where they read and discuss novels in individual groups depending on what novel they are reading. After finishing the novel, the groups choose a favorite chapter or chapters and write a play depicting that part of the story. They then act out the play for the rest of the class. Also, monthly 'Book Shares' are assigned on different genres of literature along with a project designed to expand children's love and appreciation of literature using the arts as a vehicle."

Finally, a consensual group gem:
"Administrators need to be exposed to these arts as well."
Amen to that.

— NOTES —

1. Judith Aronson, *Coming to Our Senses* Rockefeller Panel Report (New York: McGraw Hill, 1977).

2. William and Mary Esler, *Teaching Elementary Science* (Belmont, CA: Wadsworth/Thomson Learning, 2001).

3. Anna Mulrine, "Wish You had That Nose," in *Senses. U.S. News and World Report* (Jan. 13 1997).

4. Thomas E. Rowan and Lorna J. Morrow, eds., *Implementing the K–8 Curriculum and Evaluation Standards* (Reston, VA: National Council of Teachers of Mathematics, 1993).

5. Edna Doll, and M. Nelson, "Writing in Rhythm," *Rhythms Today* 1965 Silver Burdett. Reprinted by permission of Pearson Education, Inc.

6. Guy Hubbard, *Art in Action*, Book 7 (Coronado Publishers Harcourt, 1986).

7. "Trying on Turtle's Sandals," from *The Music Connection*, Grade 1, Teacher's Edition, © 1995 by Silver Burdett Ginn, Inc. Reprinted by permission of Pearson Education, Inc.

8. Vilate Raile, from poetry collected *So There* © Bookmark Press, 1942.

9. "On Being Twelve," poem by Anna Maskel, master training teacher at Southern Connecticut State University.

— FOR FURTHER READING —

Augarde, Tony. *The Oxford Guide to Word Games*. New York: Oxford University Press, 1985.

Bonica, Diana. *Writing and Art Go Hand in Hand*. Nashville, TN: Incentive Publications, 1988.

Byrom, Thomas. *Nonsense and Wonder: The Poems and Cartoons of Edward Lear*. New York: E. P. Dutton, 1977.

Carroll, L. *Jabberwocky*. New York: Warner Books, 1997.

Cipra, Barry "Cross Disciplinary Artists Know Good Math When They See It." *Science* 257 (1992): 48–49.

Colbert, Cynthia, and Rebecca Brooks. *Connections in Art* (Links to language arts, social studies, math, science, music, drama and dance). Worcester, MA: Davis Publications.

Fauth, B. "Linking the Visual Arts with Drama, Movement and Dance for the Young Child." In *Moving and Learning for the Young Child*, ed. J. Stinson. Reston, VA: AAHPERD, 1990.

Fleischman, Paul. *Joyful Noise: Poems for Two Voices*. New York: Harper and Row, 1988.

Hall, Donald, ed. *The Oxford Book of Children's Verse in America*. New York: Oxford University Press, 1985.

Higginson, William J., with Penny Horten. *The Haiku Handbook: How to Write, Share and Teach Haiku*. New York: Kodansha International, 1985.

Kagan, Andrew. *Paul Klee/Art and Music*. Ithaca, NY: Cornell University Press, 1983.

Katz, S., and J. Thomas. *Teaching Creativity by the Working Word: Language, Music and Movement*. Prentice Hall, 1992.

Koch, Kenneth, and Kate Farrell, ed. *Talking to the Sun: An Illustrated Anthology of Poems for Young People*. New York: Metropolitan Museum of Art, Henry Holt, 1985.

Kohl, Mary Ann, and Jean Potter. *Science Arts: Discovering Science through Art Expression*. Bright Ring Publishing, 1993.

Langone, John. *The Mystery of Time*. National Geographic, 2000.

Levine, Shar, and Leslie Johnstone. *The Science of Sound and Music*. New York: Sterling Publishing Co., 2000.

Milne, A. A. *When We Were Very Young*. New York: E. P. Dutton, 1961.

Prelutsky, J. *The Random House Book of Poetry for Children*. New York: Random House, 1983.

_____. *The New Kid on the Block*. New York: Greenwillow, 1984.

Renfro, Nancy, and Connie Champlin. *Story Telling with Puppets*. Chicago, IL: Chicago Press, 1985.

Rothstein, Edward. *Emblems of Mind: The Inner Life of Music and Mathematics*. New York: Times Books, 1995.

Selwyn, Douglas. *Living History: Integrative Arts Activities for Making Social Studies Meaningful*. Tucson, AZ: Zephyr Press, 1993.

Silverstein, S. *Where the Sidewalk Ends*. New York: Harper & Row, 1974.

_____. *A Light in the Attic*. New York: Harper & Row, 1981.

Van Schuyver, Jan. *Story Telling Made Easy with Puppets*. Phoenix, AZ: Onyx Press, 1993.

Williams, D. *Teaching Mathematics Through Children's Art*. Portsmouth, NH: Heineman, 1995.

Winternitz, Emanual. *Leonardo daVinci as a Musician* New Haven, CT: Yale University Press, 1982.

APPENDIX A

Multiple Intelligences Survey

Part I

Complete each section by placing a "1" next to each statement you feel accurately describes you. If you do not identify with a statement, leave the space provided blank. Then total the column in each section.

SECTION 1

_____ I enjoy categorizing things by common traits.

_____ Ecological issues are important to me.

_____ Hiking and camping are enjoyable activities.

_____ I enjoy working on a garden.

_____ I believe preserving our National Parks is important.

_____ Putting things in hierarchies makes sense to me.

_____ Animals are important in my life.

_____ My home has a recycling system in place.

_____ I enjoy studying biology, botany, and/or zoology.

_____ I spend a great deal of time outdoors.

_____ TOTAL for Section 1

SECTION 2

_____ I easily pick up on patterns.

_____ I focus in on noise and sounds.

_____ Moving to a beat is easy for me.

_____ I've always been interested in playing an instrument.

_____ The cadence of poetry intrigues me.

_____ I remember things by putting them in a rhyme.

_____ Concentration is difficult while listening to a radio or television.

_____ I enjoy many kinds of music.

_____ Musicals are more interesting than dramatic plays.

_____ Remembering song lyrics is easy for me.

_____ TOTAL for Section 2

SECTION 3

_____ I keep my things neat and orderly.

_____ Step-by-step directions are a big help.

_____ Solving problems comes easily to me.

_____ I get easily frustrated with disorganized people.

_____ I can complete calculations quickly in my head.

_____ Puzzles requiring reasoning are fun.

_____ I can't begin an assignment until all my questions are answered.

_____ Structure helps me be successful.

_____ I find working on a computer spreadsheet or database rewarding.

_____ Things have to make sense to me or I am dissatisfied.

_____ TOTAL for Section 3

SECTION 4

_____ It is important to see my role in the "big picture" of things.

_____ I enjoy discussing questions about life.

_____ Religion is important to me.

_____ I enjoy viewing art masterpieces.

_____ Relaxation and meditation exercises are rewarding.

_____ I like visiting breathtaking sites in nature.

_____ I enjoy reading ancient and modern philosophers.

_____ Learning new things is easier when I understand their value.

_____ I wonder if there are other forms of intelligent life in the universe.

_____ Studying history and ancient culture helps give me perspective.

_____ TOTAL for Section 4

SECTION 5

_____ I learn best interacting with others.

_____ The more the merrier.

_____ Study groups are very productive for me.

_____ I enjoy chat rooms.

_____ Participating in politics is important.

_____ Television and radio talk shows are enjoyable.

_____ I am a "team player."

_____ I dislike working alone.

_____ Clubs and extracurricular activities are fun.

_____ I pay attention to social issues and causes.

_____ TOTAL for Section 5

SECTION 6

_____ I enjoy making things with my hands.

_____ Sitting still for long periods of time is difficult for me.

_____ I enjoy outdoor games and sports.

_____ I value nonverbal communication such as sign language.

_____ A fit body is important for a fit mind.

_____ Arts and crafts are enjoyable pastimes.

_____ Expression through dance is beautiful.

_____ I like working with tools.

_____ I live an active lifestyle.

_____ I learn by doing.

_____ TOTAL for Section 6

SECTION 7

_____ I enjoy reading all kinds of materials.

_____ Taking notes helps me remember and understand.

_____ I faithfully contact friends through letter and/or e-mail.

_____ It is easy for me to explain my ideas to others.

_____ I keep a journal.

_____ Word puzzles like crosswords and jumbles are fun.

_____ I write for pleasure.

_____ I enjoy playing with words like puns, anagrams, and spoonerisms.

_____ Foreign languages interest me.

_____ Debates and public speaking are activities I like to participate in.

_____ TOTAL for Section 7

SECTION 8

_____ I am keenly aware of my moral beliefs.

_____ I learn best when I have an emotional attachment to the subject.

_____ Fairness is important to me.

_____ My attitude affects how I learn.

_____ Social justice issues concern me.

_____ Working alone can be just as productive as working in a group.

_____ I need to know why I should do something before I agree to do it.

_____ When I believe in something I will give 100 percent effort to it.

_____ I like to be involved in causes that help others.

_____ I am willing to protest or sign a petition to right a wrong.

_____ TOTAL for Section 8

SECTION 9

_____ I can imagine ideas in my mind.

_____ Rearranging a room is fun for me.

_____ I enjoy creating art using varied media.

_____ I remember well using graphic organizers.

_____ Performance art can be very gratifying.

_____ Spreadsheets are great for making charts, graphs, and tables.

_____ Three-dimensional puzzles bring me much enjoyment.

_____ Music videos are very simulating.

_____ I can recall things in mental pictures.

_____ I am good at reading maps and blueprints.

_____ TOTAL for Section 9

Part II

Now carry forward your total from each section and multiply by 10 below:

Section	Total Forward	Multiply	Score
1		× 10	
2		× 10	
3		× 10	
4		× 10	
5		× 10	
6		× 10	
7		× 10	
8		× 10	
9		× 10	

Part III

Now plot your scores on the bar graph provided:

100									
90									
80									
70									
60									
50									
40									
30									
20									
10									
0	Sec 1	Sec 2	Sec 3	Sec 4	Sec 5	Sec 6	Sec 7	Sec 8	Sec 9

Part IV

Section 1—This reflects your Naturalist strength.

Section 2—This suggests your Musical strength.

Section 3—This indicates your Logical strength.

Section 4—This illustrates your Existential strength.

Section 5—This shows your Interpersonal strength.

Section 6—This tells your Kinesthetic strength.

Section 7—This indicates your Verbal strength.

Section 8—This reflects your Intrapersonal strength.

Section 9—This suggests your Visual strength.

*Multiple Intelligence Inventory, <http://surfaquarium.com/miinvent.htm>. © 1999
Walter McKenzie, Surfaquarium Consulting.*

INDEX